WEBER'S
Tropical Barbecue™

WEBER'S
Tropical Barbecue™

ISLAND FLAVOURS
ON THE GRILL

LUCY KNOX

MQP

From Trudy Schuringa: thanks to Rob, Sharon, Hayley and Lucy Pollock for the use of their pool.

Published by MQ Publications Limited
12 The Ivories, 6–8 Northampton Street
London N1 2HY
Tel: 44 (0)20 7359 2244
Fax: 44 (0)20 7359 1616
email: mail@mqpublications.com
www.mqpublications.com

Produced by MQ Publications Ltd under
exclusive licence from Weber-Stephen
Products Co.

MQ Publications:
Zaro Weil, CEO & Publisher

Weber-Stephen Products Co.:
Mike Kempster Sr., Executive Vice President
Jeff Stephen, Vice President Export Sales

Recipe Credits: Lucy Knox

Recipes:
Food photography: Gareth Sambidge
Home economy: Carol Tennant
Stylist: Rachel Jukes

Location:
Location photographer: Trudy Schuringa
Stylist: Georgia Young

ISBN: 1-84061-052-7

1 3 5 7 9 0 8 6 4 2

Printed and bound in France by *Partenaires Book*®

This book contains the opinions and ideas of the
author. It is intended to provide helpful and
informative material on the subjects addressed
in this book and is sold with the understanding
that the author and publisher are not engaged
in rendering any kind of personal professional
services in this book. The author and publisher
disclaim all responsibility for any liability, loss, or
risk, personal or otherwise, which is incurred
as a consequence, directly or indirectly, of the
use and application of any of the contents of
this book.

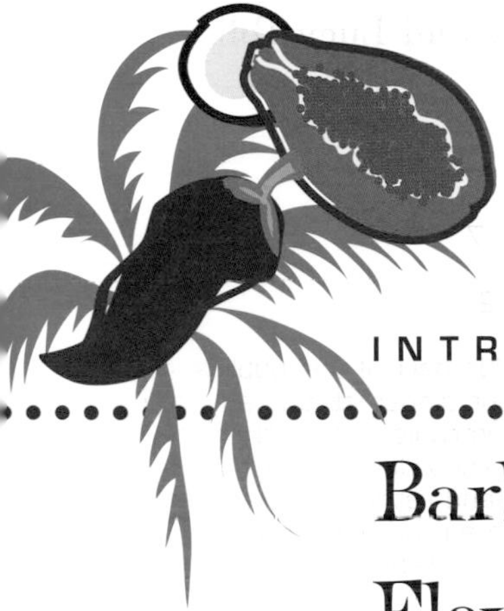

Introduction

Who would turn down the chance to enjoy freshly barbecued food on the beach of a beautiful deserted island? If that isn't an option, the next best thing is to recreate exactly that in your own back garden. Sit back, sip a fruity rum cocktail, sample some of these sensational tropical barbecue delights and allow your daydreams to whisk you away to that perfect island dream.

Open fires have always been a popular cooking method in the Tropics, from Hawaii to the West Indies. The earliest Spanish settlers in the Caribbean learned from native Indians how to cook meat over fires made from animal hides and bones. They called this "barbacoa", from which we take our modern word barbecue. Subsequent generations of immigrants from all over the world embraced this cooking technique that is so well suited to the islands, with their warm climate, lush landscapes, and sociable people.

At Hawaiian luaus, a pit is dug and lined with hot coals, after which a whole pig is lowered in and slowly roasted with herbs and spices. The ensuing parties are always extremely festive occasions, with abundant food and lavish entertainment, and are a fantastic inspiration for your own tropical feast!

Cooking on a barbie is quick, simple, easy – and a lot of fun! You get that glorious smokey flavour and those lovely sear marks on the dishes you serve. The taste and texture of sizzling, smoking barbecue food is absolutely irresistible, especially when combined with the mouth-watering spices of the tropics. Their colourful heritage means that the cuisine represents an amazing fusion of flavours, from African, to Spanish, Dutch, British, Indian, and Chinese, and with so many influences, no wonder each dish is an adventure for the tastebuds.

Barbecues mean fun and laughter, the wonderful smell of fabulous food wafting across the great outdoors, the primitive appeal of cooking over coals and the way grilling outdoors encourages family and friends to gather round, talk and join in.

In this book you'll learn how to make a range of exotic dishes, from Jamaican Jive Sea Bass and King Creole's Rockin' Lamb Kebabs, to Party-time Hot Pork Ribs and Castaway Corn with Adobo Butter. For those with a sweeter tooth, there are amazing desserts such as Monsoon Mango Wedges or Tipsy Hot Fruit Salad. There's a delicious tropical treat to tempt everyone!

The recipes are all designed to be quick and easy, simple yet stylish—perfect for capturing that laid-back tropical atmosphere in gardens, backyards, balconies or beaches. So pour yourself another Banana Daiquiri, toss some more chicken wings on the grill, and get your exotic barbecue going with a swing!

Barbecue Basics

CHARCOAL GRILLS

The secret of cooking on a charcoal kettle lies in the proper use of the lid and the vent system, along with two proven methods of positioning the charcoal briquettes. Air is drawn through the bottom vents to provide the oxygen necessary to keep the coals burning. The air heats and rises and is reflected off the lid, so it circulates around the food being cooked, eventually passing out through the top vent.

The art of charcoal barbecuing lies in mastering the fire – knowing how to set it up and how to control the temperature. Once you master that, it's easy and fun to cook entire menus and experiment with different combinations – and when you get the timing right, your guests will be able to enjoy all the food hot from the barbecue at the right time!

BUILDING THE FIRE

- **Use the right fuel:** solid hardwood charcoal briquettes are best. Look for either the square or round (also known as beads) types. Stay away from petroleum-based charcoal briquettes. They may last longer but they give off an unpleasant taste.

- **Use firelighters:** the waxy looking sticks or cubes – whenever possible, as they do not impart the chemical flavour often found when using lighter fluids. Firelighters also burn in all types of weather, ensuring a fast start to the fire. (If using lighter fluid, use it only on dry coals – never spray it on a lit fire!)

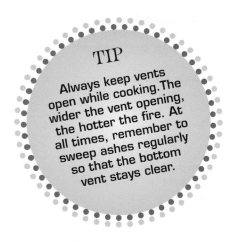

TIP

Always keep vents open while cooking. The wider the vent opening, the hotter the fire. At all times, remember to sweep ashes regularly so that the bottom vent stays clear.

LIGHTING YOUR GRILL

1. Remove the lid and open all of the air vents before building the fire. Spread the charcoal over the charcoal grate to determine how much you will need, then pile it into a mound in the centre of the grate.

2. Insert 4 firelighters (see *figure 1*), light them and let the coals catch alight and burn until they are covered with a light grey ash. This usually takes about 20 to 25 minutes. You can also use a chimney starter (see the note on page 11).

3. Use tongs to arrange the coals on the grate according to the cooking method you are going to use.

● **For Direct cooking** (see *figure 2* and page 16), you should have an even layer of hot coals across the charcoal grate.

● **For Indirect cooking** (see *figure 3* and page 17), you should have enough coals to arrange them evenly on either side of the charcoal grate.

4. Finally, place the cooking grate over the coals, put the lid on and preheat the cooking grate for about 10 minutes. The grill is now ready to use.

figure 1

figure 2

figure 3

HOW MUCH FUEL IS RIGHT?

Use the following charts for your initial settings, depending on the size of your barbecue. The best way to control the temperature of the barbecue is to adjust the number of coals. To get a hotter fire, add more coals to your initial settings. For a lower temperature, use fewer coals. This may require a little experimentation on your part, but eventually you will know what's right for your barbecue and the foods that you cook most often.

How many briquettes you need to use

BBQ kettle	Square traditional briquettes	Round charcoal beads
37cm diameter	15 each side	12 to 24 each side
47cm diameter	20 each side	28 to 56 each side
57cm diameter	25 each side	44 to 88 each side
95cm diameter	75 each side	4 to 8kg each side
Charcoal Go-Anywhere®	10 each side	12 to 24 each side

How many briquettes you need to add per hour for Indirect cooking

BBQ kettle	Number of coals per side / per hour
37cm diameter	6
47cm diameter	7
57cm diameter	8
95cm diameter	22
Charcoal Go-Anywhere®	6

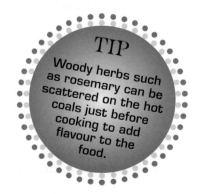

TIP
Woody herbs such as rosemary can be scattered on the hot coals just before cooking to add flavour to the food.

LIGHTING AGENTS

- **Firelighters:** Barbecue firelighters are waxy looking cubes or sticks, which are designed to light the barbecue without giving off any harmful fumes that could taint the food. Push four into the charcoal and light with a taper or a long stem match. They are easy to use, clean and safe. Only use firelighters designed for barbecues. Do not use firelighters designed for domestic fires as they contain paraffin, which will spoil the food.
- **Firelighter fluid:** If using this product you should handle with care. Please consult and follow all instructions and safety guidelines recommended by the manufacturer.

CHIMNEY STARTER

A metal canister with a handle, a chimney starter holds a supply of charcoal. Crumpled newspaper or firelighters are put on the charcoal grate and lit, the chimney starter filled with coals is positioned over the firelighters. The walls of the chimney starter focus the flames and heat onto the charcoal, decreasing the amount of time it takes for the coals to light and ash over. Once the coals are ready, simply tip the coals onto the charcoal grate and arrange them for barbecuing.

EXTINGUISHING THE FIRE

1. Before you extinguish the coals, remove all food from the cooking grate and replace the lid. Allow the barbecue to continue heating the cooking grate until any smoking stops, 10 to 15 minutes, to burn off any cooking residues. Then give the grate a good brushing with a brass-bristle brush.

2. Close the lid, all vents, and dampers to allow the barbecue to cool down.

3. Do not handle hot ashes. Wait until they are cold, and remove them so they don't attract moisture and encourage rust. Some grills are equipped with blades that sweep the ashes into ash pans or catchers. Dispose of the ashes properly in a fireproof container. Always remove the ashes before storing a charcoal barbecue.

GAS GRILLS

Gas grills have one main advantage over charcoal and that's speed. Push the ignition switch and within about 10 minutes the barbecue is up to heat and ready to use. The workings of a gas barbecue are simple. First come burners to create heat, then some type of system above the burners to help disperse the heat, such as metal bars, lava rocks, or ceramic briquettes. Above this is the cooking grate. Underneath the cooking box is a tray for collecting debris and fats.

Gas barbecues are run on Liquid Petroleum (LP) gas, which comes in two forms, butane or propane. The gas is under moderate pressure in the cylinder and is liquid. As the pressure is released the liquid vaporizes and becomes a gas.

LIGHTING YOUR GRILL

1. Check that there is enough fuel in your gas bottle (some barbecues have gauges to measure how much is left) and make sure that the burner control knobs are turned off.

2. Open the lid. Turn the gas valve on the bottle to 'on'.

3. Turn on the starter burner and light the grill according to the manufacturer's instructions using either the ignition switch or a match. When the gas flame has ignited, turn on the other burners.

4. Close the lid and preheat the grill until the thermometer reads 245 to 275°C. This takes about 10 minutes.

5. Using a brass bristle brush, clean the grate to remove any debris left over from your last barbecue.

TIP
Always read the safety instructions carefully on transporting, storing and fitting gas bottles.

6. Adjust the burner controls according to the cooking method, Direct (*figure 4*) or Indirect (*figure 5*), you are going to use. The barbecue is now ready for cooking.

figure 4   figure 5

GETTING THE RIGHT TEMPERATURE

Most gas barbecues today have burner controls that are set to Low, Medium and High, but each model uses a different temperature, so be sure to learn what those are on your model. The recipes in this book are gauged to temperatures of about 150°C for Low; 180°C for Medium; and 245 to 275°C for High. Some gas barbecues have a built-in thermometer, but if yours does not, use an oven thermometer placed on the cooking grate.

TURNING THE FIRE OFF

1. Make sure all burners are switched to 'off'. Then shut the gas down at the source.

2. When the barbecue has cooled down, preferably the next day, remove the catch pan from the bottom tray, or empty the drip tray so you don't get flare-ups or grease fires the next time you barbecue.

SMOKING

It's easy to add a more distinctive flavour to barbecued food by adding manufactured or natural flavourings to the smouldering coals, or the smoker box in the case of gas barbecues, before cooking. There are many types of flavoured woods and herbs available. They come in either chunks or chips, and should be soaked in cold water for at least 30 minutes prior to use.

● **On a charcoal barbecue:** Place the soaked chunks, chips or herbs directly on the hot coals. Add the food to the cooking grate and barbecue according to the recipe.

● **On a gas barbecue:** If your barbecue has a smoker box accessory, follow the manufacturer's instructions. If your barbecue does not have a smoker box accessory, simply place the chunks, chips or herbs in a small metal foil pan, cover with aluminium foil (poke holes in the aluminium foil to allow smoke to escape) and place directly over the heat disbursement system or the cooking grate in one corner. Turn the grill on and, as it heats up, smoke will begin to form, and will flavour the food as it cooks. Never place the food directly over the pan of smoking materials.

weber Q AND weber baby Q

The Weber® Q™ is the first gas barbecue that can act as both a fully functioning barbecue for your garden and a portable gas barbecue.

Compact, just 46cm from front to back, and 80cm from handle to handle, the porcelain-enamelled cast-iron cooking grate lets you grill up to 10 king-size steaks or 15 burgers at the same time and a deep lid can cover a whole chicken.

The Weber® Q™ and Weber® Baby Q™ (see *figure 6* and picture opposite) work in much the same way as other Weber gas barbecues with the exception that you cannot cook using the Indirect method on these grills. You can achieve a similar result by reducing the temperature to low and cooking larger cuts of meat on a roast holder. Where the cooking times and methods differ slightly than normal these are noted on the grilling charts on pages 22 to 27 and in the grilling methods noted at the start of each recipe.

figure 6

TIP

Remember, never store your barbecue indoors with the bottle attached. If properly covered, a gas barbecue can withstand the elements outside and always be ready for action.

LIGHTING WEBER® Q™ BARBECUES

1. Check that there is enough fuel in your gas bottle and that the burner control knob is turned off.

2. Open the lid and, on the Weber® Q™ gas grill, unfold the side tables.

3. Set the burner control knob to START/HI. Press the red igniter button to light the grill.

4. Close the lid and preheat the grill for about 10 minutes. The temperature will probably have reached approximately 245 to 275°C by this point.

5. Adjust the burner control knob according to the cooking method you are going to use.

EXTINGUISHING THE FIRE

1. To clean your cooking grate turn the burner to HI and leave for about 10 minutes. Then brush the cooking grate with a brass-bristle brush.

2. Make sure the burner is switched to 'off'. Then, shut the gas down at the source.

3. When the barbecue has cooled down, preferably the next day, remove the catch pan from the bottom tray, or empty the drip tray so you don't get flare-ups or grease fires the next time you barbecue.

DIRECT COOKING

The **Direct** method means that the food is cooked directly over the heat source. To ensure that foods cook evenly, turn them only once, halfway through the grilling time. Direct cooking is also the best technique for searing meats. In addition to creating a wonderful caramelized texture and flavour, searing also adds grill marks to the surface of the meat. To sear meats, place them over Direct heat for 2 to 5 minutes per side. Remember that smaller pieces of meat require less searing time, and be especially mindful of too much searing on very lean cuts of meat as they can dry out quickly. After searing, finish cooking using the method called for in the recipe.

ON CHARCOAL

1. Prepare and light the coals as instructed on pages 8 to 9. Remember, don't begin to barbecue until the coals are covered in a light grey ash. Spread the prepared coals in an even layer across the charcoal grate.

2. Set the cooking grate over the coals, put the lid on and preheat the cooking grate for about 10 minutes. Place the food on the cooking grate and cover with the lid. The food will cook directly over the heat source (see *figure 7*).

3. Do not lift the lid during cooking time, except to turn the food once halfway through and to test for readiness.

figure 7

ON GAS

1. To set up the barbecue for Direct cooking, first preheat with all burners on High. Once the barbecue is up to heat, usually about 10 minutes, adjust all burners to the temperature called for in the recipe.

2. Place the food on the cooking grate and close the lid. Again, the food will be cooked over the heat source (see *figure 8*).

3. Do not lift the lid during cooking time, except to turn the food once halfway through and to test for readiness.

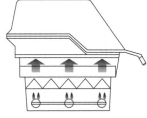

figure 8

INDIRECT COOKING

Indirect cooking is similar to roasting, but the barbecue adds flavour and texture that you can't get from the oven. The heat rises and reflects off the lid and inside surfaces of the barbecue to cook the food slowly and evenly on all sides. As in a convection oven, there is no need to turn the food over because the heat circulates around the food.

ON CHARCOAL

1. Prepare and light the coals as instructed on pages 8 to 9. Remember, don't begin to barbecue until the coals are covered in a light grey ash. Arrange the hot coals evenly on either side of the charcoal grate. Charcoal/fuel baskets or rails are accessories that keep the coals in place.

2. Place a drip pan in the centre of the charcoal grate between the coals to catch drippings. The drip pan also helps prevent flare-ups when cooking fatty foods such as duck, goose or fatty roasts. For longer cooking times, add water to the drip pan to keep the fat and food particles from burning.

3. Set the cooking grate over the coals, put the lid on and preheat the cooking grate for about 10 minutes. Place the food on the cooking grate over the drip pan and between the heat zones above the coals (see *figure 9*).

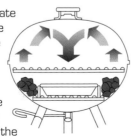

figure 9

4. Close the lid and open it only to add coals for longer cooking times, baste the meat or check for readiness.

ON GAS

1. Preheat the barbecue with all burners on High. Once the barbecue is up to heat, usually about 10 minutes, adjust the burners to the temperature called for in the recipe, turning off the burner(s) directly below the food.

2. Place the food on the cooking grate between the heat zones (see *figure 10*). For best results with roasts, poultry or large cuts of meat, use a roasting rack set inside a metal foil pan to catch the drippings.

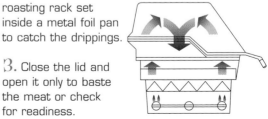

3. Close the lid and open it only to baste the meat or check for readiness.

figure 10

BARBECUE HINTS AND TIPS

Stating the Obvious
Always make sure the barbecue is up to temperature before beginning to cook. For charcoal grilling, the charcoal should have a light grey ash on it for a good hot fire, which takes between 20 and 25 minutes. Use a chimney starter for best results. For gas grilling, first, open the lid (unfold the work surfaces on the Q™ gas grill), turn on the gas source, turn the burner control knobs to High (START/HI on the Q™ gas grill) and push a button to ignite the burner(s). Shut the lid, leave for about 10 minutes and you're ready to barbecue.

Down, Boy
Always cook with the lid of your barbecue down or on. This will reduce the chances of flare-ups and cook your food faster and more evenly. While cooking, resist the urge to open the lid to check on your dinner every couple of minutes. Every time you lift the lid, heat escapes causing your food to take longer to cook.

Don't Flip Out
Unless the recipe calls for it, flip your food just once.

Easy on the Squeeze
Resist the urge to use your spatula to press down on foods such as burgers or steaks. In doing this you'll only succeed in squeezing out all of the flavour, not making it cook faster.

Moisturize
A light coating of oil will help brown your food evenly and keep it from sticking to the cooking grate. Always brush or spray oil on your food, not the cooking grate.

Forget the Fork
Poking meat with a fork whilst cooking causes juices and flavour to escape and dries out your food. Just use the fork for lifting food from the grill and nothing more.

Cut It Out
Trim excess fat from steaks, chops and roasts leaving no more than a scant 5mm thick layer.

Adjust to Your Environment
Grilling times listed in the recipes are approximate. Allow more time on cold or windy days or at higher altitudes.

Procrastinate
When using a marinade or glaze with a high sugar content or other ingredients that burn easily, brush on food only during the last 10 to 15 minutes of cooking.

Is Dinner Ready Yet?
A kitchen timer and an instant-read

thermometer are your best defences against overcooked foods. Use the thermometer to check on readiness in roasts, or thick cuts of meat, but never leave it in the food while cooking.

- **Every Time You Grill**
  Do the burn off. On a gas grill, turn all of the burners on high, close the lid, leave

for about 10 to 15 minutes, then brush the cooking grates thoroughly with a brass-bristle, long-handled grill brush (use a steel brush on cast-iron grates). For a charcoal grill, unless you have a very hot fire going when you are finished barbecuing, it's easier to clean your cooking grate just before you begin cooking – after the grate has pre-heated.

SAFE SIZZLE

- Always keep the barbecue at least 3m away from any combustible materials including the house, garage and fences.

- Do not use the grill indoors or under a covered patio, open garage door or carport.

- Keep children and pets away from a hot barbecue at all times.

- Do not add lighter fluid to a lit fire.

- Make sure the barbecue is sturdy; do not use if it wobbles, or is otherwise unstable. Always stand the barbecue on a level surface.

- Use heat-resistant barbecue mitts at all times while cooking. Use long-handled tongs to turn the food.

- Do not spray oil on a hot cooking grate; oil the food instead.

- Do not use water to extinguish a flare-up. Close the lid (and all vents on a charcoal grill) to reduce the oxygen flow and eliminate flare-ups. If necessary, turn a gas grill off at the source. Keep a fire extinguisher handy in case of a mishap.

- Do not store propane tanks indoors or in the garage.

- Do not line the bottom of a barbecue or cover the cooking grate with foil. This obstructs airflow and also collects grease, which can result in flare-ups.

- When finished barbecuing, close the lid and all vents on a charcoal barbecue; close the lid and turn off all burners and the LP tank or source on a gas grill. Make sure that hot coals are fully extinguished before leaving the barbecue site.

FOOD SAFETY

● Defrost meat, fish and poultry only in the refrigerator, never at room temperature.

● Allow meats to come to room temperature before cooking, but do not do so in a room that is over 21°C. Do not place raw food in direct sunlight or near a heat source.

● When using a sauce during barbecuing, divide it in half and keep one part separate for serving with the finished dish. Use the other half for basting the meat; do not use this as a sauce for serving. If using a marinade that was used on raw meats, fish or poultry, boil it vigorously for at least 1 full minute before using it as a baste or sauce.

● Do not place cooked food on the same dish that the raw food was placed on prior to cooking.

● Wash all dishes, plates, cooking utensils, barbecuing tools and work surfaces that have come into contact with raw meats or fish with hot soapy water. Wash your hands thoroughly after handling raw meats or fish.

● Chill any leftover cooked food from the barbecue once it has cooled.

● Always barbecue minced meats to at least 71°C (77°C for poultry), the temperature for medium (well-done) readiness.

ACCESSORIES

For best results, use the right tools when barbecuing. Here is a list of some of the essentials:

● Wide metal spatula – used for turning chicken pieces, vegetables and smaller pieces of food.

● Long-handled grill brush – preferably with brass bristles, to keep the grates clean without scratching the porcelain enamel. A steel-bristle brush is best for cleaning cast-iron grates.

● Basting brush – used for basting food with a marinade or oil. Best with natural bristles (nylon bristles will melt if they touch the cooking grate) and a long handle.

● Long-handled tongs – used for turning sausages, shellfish, kebabs, etc.

● Long-handled fork – used for lifting cooked roasts and whole poultry from the barbecue.

● Barbecue mitts/oven gloves – these should be long-sleeved, flame-resistant gloves to protect your hands and forearms.

● Skewers – wooden or metal skewers are excellent for holding small pieces of meat, fish or vegetables and make it easy to turn food quickly on the barbecue, ensuring faster cooking. Remember to soak wooden skewers, if using them, in cold water for at least 30 minutes before adding the food.

● Meat thermometer – used for best results every time, a thermometer takes the guesswork out of judging if food is cooked.

● Timer – an excellent tool, so you don't have to watch the clock and can continue preparing other parts of the meal while the food is cooking.

● Foil drip pans – these keep the base of the barbecue clean and gather fats and juices that fall from the food during cooking.

● Roast holder – when cooking large cuts of meat and poultry on a gas barbecue, a roast holder in a foil pan will catch the drippings and reduce the chance of flare-ups.

TIP

Long-handled equipment makes the job safer.

BARBECUE GUIDES

The following thicknesses, weights and barbecue times are meant to be general guidelines rather than firm rules and you may notice that recipe times vary in comparison. When following a recipe, always follow the specific instructions. Cooking times are affected by wind, outside temperature and desired degree of cooking.

KEY TO METHOD OF COOKING

In the following fish, meat, poultry, vegetable and fruit cooking charts the approximate cooking time is followed by the barbecue method. These methods are also referred to throughout the book. Note: when cooking on Weber® Q™ or Weber® Baby Q™ always turn food once halfway through cooking, even if using a roast holder.

DL	Direct Low Heat
DM	Direct Medium Heat
DH	Direct High Heat
IL	Indirect Low Heat
IM	Indirect Medium Heat
IH	Indirect High Heat

Fish & Seafood	Thickness/Weight	Grilling Time for Gas/Charcoal	Grilling Time for Weber® Q™ and Weber® Baby Q™
Fish fillet or steak	5mm to 1cm thick	3 to 5 minutes DH	3 to 5 minutes DH
	1cm to 2.5cm thick	5 to 10 minutes DH	5 to 10 minutes DH
	2.5cm to 3cm thick	10 to 12 minutes DH	10 to 12 minutes DH
Fish, whole	450g	15 to 20 minutes IM	15 to 20 minutes DM
	900g to 1.1kg	20 to 30 minutes IM	20 to 30 minutes DM
	1.4kg	30 to 45 minutes IM	
Fish kebab	2.5cm thick	8 to 10 minutes DM	8 to 10 minutes DM
Prawn		2 to 4 minutes DH	2 to 4 minutes DH
Scallop		3 to 6 minutes DH	3 to 6 minutes DH
Mussel (discard any that do not open)		5 to 6 minutes DH	5 to 6 minutes DH
Clam (discard any that do not open)		8 to 10 minutes DH	8 to 10 minutes DH
Oyster		3 to 5 minutes DH	3 to 5 minutes DH
Lobster tail		7 to 11 minutes DM	7 to 11 minutes DM

Note: General rule for grilling fish: 4 to 5 minutes per 1cm thickness; 8 to 10 minutes per 2.5cm thickness.

Beef	Thickness/Weight	Grilling Time for Gas/Charcoal	Grilling Time for Weber® Q™ and Weber® Baby Q™
Steak: sirloin, T-bone or rib	2.5cm thick	6 to 8 minutes DH	6 to 8 minutes DH
	3cm thick	8 to 10 minutes DH	8 to 10 minutes DH
	4cm thick	12 to 16 minutes total; sear 8 to 10 minutes cook 4 to 6 minutes IH	12 to 16 minutes total; sear 8 to 10 minutes DH, cook 4 to 6 minutes DL
	5cm thick	18 to 22 minutes total; sear 8 to 10 minutes DH, cook 10 to 12 minutes IH	
Skirt steak	5mm to 1cm thick	4 to 6 minutes DH	4 to 6 minutes DH
Flank steak	650g to 900g 2cm thick	8 to 10 minutes DH	8 to 10 minutes DH
Kebab	2.5cm to 4cm cubes	7 to 8 minutes DH	7 to 8 minutes DH
Tenderloin, whole	1.5kg to 1.75kg	35 to 50 minutes total; sear 15 minutes DM, cook 20 to 30 minutes IM	45 to 50 minutes sear 12 minutes DH (turn 4 times), cook 33 to 38 minutes DL
Minced beef burger	2cm thick	8 to 10 minutes DH	8 to 10 minutes DM
Rib roast (prime rib), boneless	2.25kg to 2.75kg	1¼ to 1¾ hours IM	1½ to 2 hours DL (on roasting rack) – on Q™ grill only
Strip loin roast, boneless	1.75kg to 2.25kg	45 to 60 minutes total; sear 2 to 4 minutes DH, cook 45 to 60 minutes IM	
Veal loin chop	2.5cm thick	6 to 8 minutes DH	6 to 8 minutes DH

Note: All cooking times are for medium-rare readiness, except minced beef (medium).

Safe Cooking Temperature for Beef

Cook beef roasts and steaks to 62°C for medium rare (71°C for medium) / cook minced beef to at least 71°C.

Pork	Thickness/Weight	Grilling Time for Gas/Charcoal	Grilling Time for Weber® Q™ and Weber® Baby Q™
Bratwurst, fresh		20 to 25 minutes DM	25 to 30 minutes DL
Bratwurst, pre-cooked		10 to 12 minutes DM	10 to 12 minutes DM
Pork chop, boneless or bone-in	1cm thick	5 to 7 minutes DH	5 to 7 minutes DH
	2cm thick	6 to 8 minutes DH	6 to 8 minutes D
	2.5cm thick	8 to 10 minutes DM	8 to 10 minutes DM
	3cm to 4cm thick	10 to 12 minutes total; sear 6 minutes DH, cook 4 to 6 minutes IM	14 to 18 minutes total; sear 8 minutes DH, cook 6 to 10 minutes DL
Loin roast, boneless	1kg	40 to 45 minutes DM	
Loin roast, bone-in	1.25kg to 2.25kg	$1^1/_4$ to $1^3/_4$ hours IM	$1^1/_4$ to $1^3/_4$ hours DL (on roasting rack) – on Q™ only
Pork shoulder, boneless	2.25kg to to 2.75kg	$3^1/_2$ to 4 hours DL	
Pork, minced burger	2cm thick	8 to 10 minutes DM	8 to 10 minutes DM
Ribs, baby back	700g to 900g	$1^1/_2$ to 2 hours IL	$1^1/_4$ to $1^1/_2$ hours DL (on rib rack) – on Q™ only
Ribs, spareribs	1.25kg to 2.25kg	$2^1/_2$ to 3 hours IL	$1^1/_4$ to $1^1/_2$ hours DL (on rib rack) – on Q™ only
Tenderloin, whole	350g to 450g	15 to 20 minutes DM	25 to 30 minutes total; sear 10 minutes DH (turn 3 times), then cook 15 to 20 minutes DL

Safe Cooking Temperature for Pork

Cook all pork to 71°C.

Safe Cooking Temperature for Lamb

Cook lamb to 62°C for medium rare (71°C for medium) / cook minced lamb to 71°C.

Safe Cooking Temperature for Poultry

Cook whole poultry to 82°C / cook minced poultry to 74°C / cook chicken breasts to 77°C / cook duck and goose to 82°C.

Lamb	Thickness/Weight	Grilling Time for Gas/Charcoal	Grilling Time for Weber® Q™ and Weber® Baby Q™
Chop: loin, rib, shoulder, or sirloin	2cm to 3cm thick	8 to 12 minutes DM	8 to 12 minutes DM
Leg of lamb, butterflied	1.25kg to 1.5kg	$1^1/_4$ to $1^1/_2$ hours total; sear 10 to 15 minutes DM, cook 1 to $1^1/_4$ hours IM	
Rib crown roast	1.25kg to 1.75kg	1 to $1^1/_4$ hours IM	
Minced lamb burger	2cm thick	8 to 10 minutes DM	8 to 10 minutes DM
Rack of lamb	450g to 700g	20 to 30 minutes DM	20 to 30 minutes DM

Note: All cooking times are for medium-rare readiness, except minced lamb (medium).

Poultry	Thickness/Weight	Grilling Time for Gas/Charcoal	Grilling Time for Weber® Q™ and Weber® Baby Q™
Chicken breast, boneless, skinless	175g	8 to 12 minutes DM	8 to 12 minutes DM
Chicken thigh, boneless, skinless	115g	8 to 10 minutes DH	8 to 10 minutes DH
Chicken pieces, bone-in breast/wing		30 to 40 minutes IM	30 to 40 minutes DL
Chicken pieces, bone-in leg/thigh		40 to 50 minutes IM	40 to 50 minutes DL
Chicken, whole	1.5kg to 2.25kg	1 to $1^1/_2$ hours IM	1 to $1^1/_2$ hours DL (on roasting rack) – on Q™ grill only
Chicken kebab	2.5cm thick	6 to 8 minutes DM	6 to 8 minutes DM
Cornish game hen	700g to 900g	30 to 45 minutes IM	30 to 35 minutes DL
Turkey breast, boneless	1.25kg	1 to $1^1/_4$ hours IM	
Turkey, whole, unstuffed	4.5kg to 5kg	$1^3/_4$ to $2^1/_2$ hours IM	
	5.5kg to 6.5kg	$2^1/_4$ to 3 hours IM	
	6.75kg to 7.75kg	$2^3/_4$ to $3^3/_4$ hours IM	
	8kg to 10kg	$3^1/_2$ to 4 hours IM	
Duck breast, boneless	200g to 225g	12 to 15 minutes DL	12 to 15 minutes DL
Duck, whole	2.25kg to 2.75kg	40 minutes IH	

Vegetables	Grilling Time for Gas/Charcoal	Grilling Time for Weber® Q™ and Weber® Baby Q™
Artichoke, whole	boil 12 to 15 minutes; cut in half and grill 4 to 6 minutes DM	boil 12 to 15 minutes; cut in half and grill 4 to 6 minutes DM
Asparagus	6 to 8 minutes DM	6 to 8 minutes DM
Aubergine, 1cm slices	8 to 10 minutes DM	8 to 10 minutes DM
Aubergine, halved	12 to 15 minutes DM	12 to 15 minutes DM
Beetroot	1 to 1½ hours IM	1 to 1½ hours DL
Corn, husked	10 to 15 minutes DM	10 to 12 minutes DM
Corn, in husk	25 to 30 minutes DM	25 to 30 minutes DM
Courgette, 1cm slices	6 to 8 minutes DM	6 to 8 minutes DM
Courgette, halved	6 to 10 minutes DM	6 to 10 minutes DM
Fennel, 5mm slices	10 to 12 minutes DM	10 to 12 minutes DM
Garlic, whole	45 to 60 minutes IM	45 to 60 minutes DL
Green bean, whole	8 to 10 minutes DM	8 to 10 minutes DM
Spring onion, whole	3 to 4 minutes DM	3 to 4 minutes DM
Leek, halved	steam 4 to 5 minutes; grill 3 to 5 minutes DM	steam 4 to 5 minutes; grill 3 to 5 minutes DM
Mushroom: shiitake or button	8 to 10 minutes DM	8 to 10 minutes DM
Mushroom: portabello	10 to 15 minutes DM	10 to 15 minutes DM
Onion, halved	35 to 40 minutes IM	
Onion, 1cm slices	8 to 12 minutes DM	8 to 12 minutes DM
Pepper, whole	10 to 15 minutes DM	10 to 12 minutes DM
Pepper, 5mm slices	6 to 8 minutes DM	6 to 8 minutes DM
Potato, whole	45 to 60 minutes IM	45 to 60 minutes DL
Potato, 1cm slices	14 to 16 minutes DM	14 to 16 minutes DM
Potato: new, halved	15 to 20 minutes DM	15 to 20 minutes DM
Pumpkin (1.25kg), halved	1½ to 2 hours IM	1½ to 2 hours DL
Squash: acorn (450g), halved	1 to 1¼ hours IM	1 to 1¼ hours DL
Squash: butternut (900g), halved	50 to 55 minutes IM	50 to 55 minutes DL
Squash: patty pan	10 to 12 minutes DM	10 to 12 minutes DM
Squash: yellow, 1cm slices	6 to 8 minutes DM	6 to 8 minutes DM
Squash: yellow, halved	6 to 10 minutes DM	6 to 10 minutes DM
Sweet potato, whole	50 to 60 minutes IM	50 to 60 minutes DL
Sweet potato, 5mm slices	8 to 10 minutes DM	8 to 10 minutes DM

Vegetables	Grilling Time for Gas/Charcoal	Grilling Time for Weber® Q™ and Weber® Baby Q™
Tomato: garden, 1cm slices	2 to 4 minutes DM	2 to 4 minutes DM
Tomato: garden, halved	6 to 8 minutes DM	6 to 8 minutes DM
Tomato: plum, halved	6 to 8 minutes DM	6 to 8 minutes DM
Tomato: plum, whole	8 to 10 minutes DM	8 to 10 minutes DM

Fruit	Grilling Time for Gas/Charcoal	Grilling Time for Weber® Q™ and Weber® Baby Q™
Apple, whole	35 to 40 minutes IM	
Apple, 1cm thick slices	4 to 6 minutes DM	4 to 6 minutes DM
Apricot, halved, pit removed	6 to 8 minutes DM	6 to 8 minutes DM
Banana, halved lengthways	6 to 8 minutes DM	6 to 8 minutes DM
Nectarine, halved lengthways, pit removed	8 to 10 minutes DM	8 to 10 minutes DM
Peach, halved lengthways, pit removed	8 to 10 minutes DM	8 to 10 minutes DM
Pear, halved lengthways	10 to 12 minutes DM	10 to 12 minutes DM
Pineapple, peeled and cored, 1cm slices or 2.5cm wedges	5 to 10 minutes DM	5 to 10 minutes DM
Strawberry	4 to 5 minutes DM	4 to 5 minutes DM

Note: Grilling times for fruit will depend on ripeness.

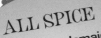

ALL SPICE

Also known as Jamaican pepper, it is a dried aromatic berry from an evergreen tree native to the West Indies and South America. It grows prolifically in Jamaica, hence its alternative name, and is mostly associated with Caribbean cuisine where it is widely used in marinades, pickles and salt beef and pork dishes.

HOT PEPPERS

A huge range of hot peppers are grown in tropical regions, ranging from fairly mild to extremely hot varieties. A large number are found in Central America and the Caribbean including the Scotch bonnet, habanero and jalapeño. All these peppers are hot but the habanero is said to be the hottest. They are used in many Caribbean dishes where heat is needed, including salsas, marinades and chutneys.

Flavours

MANGO

This is a large tropical fruit with a distinct aroma and flavour. Originally native to India it was introduced to the West Indies in the 18th century and then later into Hawaii. Sweet and juicy, mangoes are very popular. They are eaten as a fruit and also used as an accompaniment to chicken, fish or other meat dishes as well as in chutneys.

COCONUT

Widely cultivated throughout the tropics including Hawaii and the Pacific Islands, coconut is the fruit of the coconut palm. It has a variety of uses ranging from coconut oil to using the hard shells for bowls. The meat can be used fresh or dried in many recipes such as chicken and shellfish stews, while the milk is used to flavour curries and fish marinades.

CLOVES

Cloves are immature unopened flower buds from a tree growing near tropical seashores. They are indigenous to the Spice Islands of Indonesia but are now found in the West Indies and Malaysia. Cloves have a sweet and pungent flavour and feature in both sweet and savoury dishes including rich meat dishes, marinades and chutneys.

LIME

This citrus fruit is closely related to the lemon, but is smaller, juicier and more fragrant. Limes are cultivated in tropical areas and are often used in Caribbean recipes, including fish and meat stews, chicken dishes, jams, sorbets and even cocktails.

CHAPTER ONE

Island
Light Bites

Tangy Lemon Prawn Kebabs

Gas Direct High heat / **Weber® Q™** Direct High / **Charcoal** Direct
Prep time 15 minutes / **Grilling time** 4 to 6 minutes / **Serves** 4

**36 raw jumbo prawns,
  heads removed, shelled
  and deveined**
**Grated rind and juice of
  3 lemons**
**1 tablespoon smoked
  paprika**
**4 tablespoons olive oil, plus
  extra for brushing**

For the salad:
**500g fresh or frozen broad
  beans**
1 red onion, finely chopped
1 garlic clove, crushed
**2 tablespoons chopped
  fresh mint**
**2 tablespoons chopped
  fresh coriander**
2 tablespoons olive oil
**Salt and freshly ground
  black pepper**

1. Soak 12 wooden skewers in cold water for about 30 minutes. Remove them from the water and pat dry before using. Put the prawns in a non-metallic dish and add the lemon rind and juice, smoked paprika and olive oil. Stir well, so the prawns are evenly coated, then leave to stand for 5 minutes to allow the flavours to infuse.

2. Meanwhile, cook the broad beans in a saucepan of boiling water until tender. Drain well, rinse with cold water and remove the skins. Mix with the remaining ingredients to make the salad, and season with salt and pepper.

3. Remove the prawns from the marinade (and discard the marinade). Thread the prawns on to the skewers, leaving space between the prawns. Brush with olive oil, season with salt and pepper and barbecue over Direct High heat for 4 to 6 minutes until the prawns turn pink (the exact time depends on the size of the prawns) turning once halfway through.

4. Divide the salad among four plates and serve the prawns stacked on top.

TIP
Alternatively, try using the zest and juice of a lime instead of the lemon for an extra tropical twist.

Courgette & Crab Parcels

Gas Direct High heat / **Weber® Q™** Direct High heat / **Charcoal** Direct
Prep time 15 minutes + 1 hour chilling / **Grilling time** 8 to 10 minutes / **Serves** 4

400g cold cooked roughly mashed potato (made without milk or butter)
1 medium egg white
1 tablespoon each snipped fresh chives and coriander
2 (43g) cans dressed crab
¼ teaspoon habanero hot sauce
Plain flour for dusting
1 large courgette, trimmed and cut into long strips (using a potato peeler)
A little olive oil for brushing
Salt

1. Tip the roughly mashed potato (if it's too smooth the crab cakes will become too soft to hold together) into a bowl and beat in the egg white, chives and coriander, dressed crab, salt and habanero sauce. Cover with clingfilm and chill for about an hour to firm. Soak 12 wooden skewers in cold water for 30 minutes. Remove from the water and pat dry before using.

2. Tip the crab mixture onto a lightly floured board, and, with floured hands, divide into four portions, then shape each portion into three small rounds. Wrap each round with a courgette strip and secure with a skewer.

3. Lightly brush the cakes on both sides with olive oil and barbecue over Direct High heat for 6 to 8 minutes (8 to 10 minutes on Weber® Q™ gas grills), or until cooked, turning carefully once halfway through, using a spatula.

TIP
These delicious Crab Parcels are great when served with Coconut & Turmeric Mayonnaise (see page 44).

Sunshine Sweet Potato Wedges
with Red Pepper Salsa

Gas Direct Medium heat / **Weber® Q™** Direct Medium / **Charcoal** Direct
Prep time 15 minutes / **Grilling time** 10 to 15 minutes / **Serves** 4

For the salsa:
**3 red peppers, grilled until
the skins are blistered,
then peeled, seeded and
finely chopped**
2 garlic cloves, crushed
**3 spring onions, trimmed
and finely chopped**
**1 red jalapeño pepper, cored,
seeded and finely chopped**
2 tablespoons olive oil

For the sweet potato wedges:
**900g sweet potatoes,
unpeeled and scrubbed**
5 tablespoons olive oil
1 teaspoon smoked paprika
**Sea salt and freshly ground
black pepper**

1. Put all the ingredients for the salsa in a bowl and stir together. Set aside.

2. Cut the potatoes first in half, then into even-sized wedges. Mix together the olive oil, paprika, salt and pepper, and toss the potato wedges in this mix.

3. Using tongs, carefully arrange the potato wedges on the grill and barbecue over Direct Medium heat for 10 to 15 minutes, or until golden brown, crisp and cooked all the way through, turning once. Transfer the potato wedges to a large platter and serve hot with the red pepper salsa.

1 part peach brandy
1 part white Cuban rum
**1 teaspoon freshly squeezed
lime juice**
Pinch of sugar

Cuban Peach

Shake all ingredients thoroughly in a cocktail shaker with cracked ice. Strain into a cocktail glass half-filled with crushed ice. Float two thin slices of peach and a sprig of mint on the top to decorate.

King Creole's Rockin' Lamb Kebabs

Gas Direct Medium heat / **Weber® Q™** Direct Medium / **Charcoal** Direct
Prep time 25 minutes + overnight marinating / **Grilling time** 8 to 10 minutes / **Serves** 4

1 teaspoon dried oregano
3 tablespoons chopped
  fresh coriander
2 garlic cloves, crushed
2 teaspoons creole spice
  blend
500g lean lamb mince
Oil for brushing
Salt and freshly ground
  black pepper

1. Soak eight wooden skewers in cold water for
30 minutes. Remove them from the water and pat
dry before using. Mix the herbs, garlic and creole spice
blend with the minced lamb and plenty of salt and pepper.
Divide the mixture into eight portions, moulding the meat
around the skewers like koftas. Leave the skewers in the
fridge overnight to firm up.

2. Barbecue the lamb kebabs over Direct Medium heat
for 8 to 10 minutes, turning once, or until cooked
through. Serve with a bowl of freshly cooked white rice.

TIP
You can buy good creole spice blends from most shops and supermarkets. If you are unable to buy creole spice you can make your own by combining black peppercorns, ground cayenne, garlic, oregano, onion powder, paprika, sea salt and thyme.

Puerto Rican Crayfish
with Zingy Garlic & Lime Dip

Gas Direct High heat / **Weber® Q™** Direct High heat / **Charcoal** Direct
Prep time 15 minutes + 15 minutes marinating / **Grilling time** 4 to 7 minutes / **Serves** 4

24 raw shelled crayfish
4 tablespoons olive oil
2 teaspoons reaedy-made adobo rub

For the garlic & lime dip:
2 garlic cloves, crushed
2 hot red peppers, trimmed, cored, seeded and finely sliced
2 teaspoons salt
200ml fresh lime juice

1. Tip the crayfish into a large dish. Mix together the olive oil and adobo rub, and pour over the crayfish. Stir well so that they are evenly coated, then cover and chill for 15 minutes to allow the flavours to infuse.

2. Remove the crayfish from the marinade (and discard the marinade). Carefully arrange on the cooking grate and barbecue over Direct High heat for 4 to 7 minutes until they turn pink, turning once halfway through cooking.

3. Put all the ingredients for the garlic and lime dip in a bowl and stir together, then transfer to a serving bowl.

4. Serve the crayfish on a platter with the dip on the side. You may wish to pass a few cocktail sticks or dipping forks around so friends can dip in easily!

TIP
To make your own adobo rub, blend together 1 teaspoon each of onion powder, garlic powder and dried oregano, and a pinch of salt and pepper.

Chargrilled Pumpkin Chompers
with Spicy Jerk Seasoning

Gas Direct Medium heat / **Weber® Q™** Direct Medium / **Charcoal** Direct
Prep time 15 minutes / **Grilling time** 8 to 10 minutes / **Serves** 4

8 tablespoons olive oil
3 teaspoons ready-made dry Jamaican jerk seasoning
1.5kg piece of pumpkin, seeded, cut into wedges and peeled

1. Mix the olive oil and jerk seasoning together in a bowl and brush over both sides of the pumpkin wedges.

2. Barbecue the pumpkin wedges over Direct Medium heat for 8 to 10 minutes, or until the wedges are tender. Serve immediately.

1 small banana, peeled and sliced
1 part rum
1 part golden rum
¹/₂ part creme de banane
¹/₂ part freshly squeezed lime juice
¹/₂ part coconut milk
1 teaspoon sugar syrup

Banana Daiquiri

Blend all ingredients with crushed ice until smooth. Pour into a large, chilled Boston glass. Add a few ice cubes. Decorate with a large twist of banana leaf.

CHAPTER TWO

From The Ocean

Island Fish Patties
with Coconut & Turmeric Mayo on the side

Gas Direct High heat / **Weber® Q™** Direct High heat / **Charcoal** Direct
Prep time 10 minutes + 30 minutes chilling / **Grilling time** 8 to 10 minutes / **Serves** 4

450g skinless cod fillets
Grated rind of 1 lime
1cm piece fresh root ginger,
  peeled
Small bunch of fresh
  coriander leaves
1 hot red pepper, halved
  and seeded
2 tablespoons plain flour
Olive oil for brushing

For the mayo:
75ml coconut milk
1 teaspoon ground turmeric
150ml mayonnaise
Salt and freshly ground
  black pepper

1. Put the cod fillets, lime rind, ginger, coriander, hot pepper and flour in a blender and blend to make a thick, smooth mixture. Tip on to a board and shape into eight fish burgers. Cover with clingfilm and chill for 30 minutes to firm.

2. Heat the coconut milk in a small saucepan with the turmeric. When just boiling, mix well and remove from the heat. Leave to cool, then stir into the mayonnaise with a little salt and pepper.

3. Brush the burgers lightly with olive oil and cook over Direct High heat for 8 to 10 minutes, turning very carefully once.

TIP
The Weber Style Fish Turner makes turning fish burgers very simple.

Sweet Hot Pepper Scallops
with Summery Mango Salsa

Gas Direct High heat / **Weber® Q™** Direct High heat / **Charcoal** Direct
Prep time 10 minutes / **Grilling time** 4 to 5 minutes / **Serves** 4

12 large fresh scallops, trimmed
2 tablespoons sweet hot pepper (chilli) sauce
Juice of 2 limes
2 tablespoons olive oil
1 heart of romaine or cos lettuce, washed and shredded, to serve

For the mango salsa:
1 mango, peeled, stoned and finely chopped
2 spring onions, trimmed and finely chopped
1 habanero pepper or Scotch bonnet pepper, trimmed, cored, seeded and finely chopped
10cm piece cucumber, halved, seeded and finely chopped
4 tablespoons chopped fresh coriander
Salt

1. Put the scallops, hot pepper (chilli) sauce, lime juice and olive oil in a large bowl and stir gently.

2. Put all the ingredients for the mango salsa in another bowl and stir together. Add salt to taste. Cover with clingfilm and set aside until needed.

3. Remove the scallops (and discard any leftover marinade). Carefully arrange the scallops on the cooking grate, making sure they don't fall through, and barbecue over Direct High heat for 4 to 5 minutes, turning once, until just tender.

4. Arrange the shredded lettuce on four plates and serve the scallops on top with a spoonful of mango salsa.

TIP
Scotch bonnet peppers are about 2.5cm long, look like a squashed Chinese lantern and pack a powerful punch. They are grown in the Caribbean and can be pale yellow, green, orange or red with a hot, fruity, smoky flavour. Perfect for salsas and curries.

Red Snapper with Fiery Scotch Bonnet & Red Pepper Marinade

Gas Indirect Medium heat / **Weber® Q™** Direct Medium / **Charcoal** Indirect / **Prep time** 15 minutes, plus 30 minutes marinating / **Grilling time** 10 to 20 minutes / **Serves** 2

**2 small whole red snapper,
weighing about 200g
each before scaled,
gutted and fins trimmed**
Olive oil for brushing
Fresh coriander to garnish

For the marinade
**1 Scotch bonnet pepper,
trimmed, cored, seeded
and chopped**
1 onion, finely chopped
**2 red peppers, seeded and
finely chopped**
Juice of 2 lemons
A generous pinch of salt
**3 tablespoons chopped
fresh coriander**

1. Rinse the fish inside and out and pat dry with kitchen paper. Make three slashes on both sides of the fish. Mix together all the ingredients for the marinade and use to brush liberally inside and outside the fish. Pour over the remaining marinade, cover with clingfilm and chill for 30 minutes.

2. Remove the fish from the marinade (and discard the marinade). Brush the outside of the fish with the olive oil and barbecue over Indirect Medium heat for 15 to 20 minutes (or Direct Medium for 10 to 15 minutes on Weber® Q™ gas grills) turning once halfway through. Serve with crusty bread.

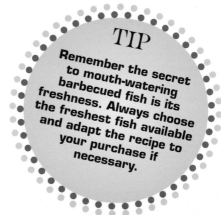

TIP
Remember the secret to mouth-watering barbecued fish is its freshness. Always choose the freshest fish available and adapt the recipe to your purchase if necessary.

Aloha Shrimps
with Mango & Papaya Mojo

Gas Direct Medium heat / **Weber® Q™** Direct Medium heat / **Charcoal** Direct
Prep time 15 minutes / **Grilling time** 4 to 7 minutes / **Serves** 4

36 raw shrimps or large prawns, heads removed, shelled and deveined
Juice of 2 limes
2 tablespoons sweet hot pepper (chilli) sauce
Oil for brushing

For the mango & papaya mojo:
1 mango, peeled, stoned and finely chopped
1 papaya, peeled, seeded and finely chopped
2 spring onions, trimmed and finely chopped
Juice of 1/2 lemon
2 tablespoons chopped fresh coriander

1. Soak 12 wooden skewers in cold water for about 30 minutes. Remove them from the water and pat dry before using. Put the shrimps in a non-metallic dish. Mix together lime juice and hot pepper (chilli) sauce and pour over the shrimps. Stir so that they are evenly coated then leave to stand for 5 minutes to allow the flavours to infuse.

2. Put all the ingredients for the mango and papaya mojo in a bowl and stir together, then transfer to a serving bowl and set aside until needed.

3. Remove the shrimps from the marinade (and discard the marinade). Thread the shrimps on to the soaked skewers and brush with a little oil, then barbecue over Direct Medium heat for 4 to 7 minutes until they turn pink, turning once halfway through cooking.

TIP
The exact cooking time for the shrimps depends on their size; the bigger they are, the longer they need.

Ocean Tuna Burgers
with Mango & Coriander Mayo

Gas Direct High heat / **Weber® Q™** Direct High heat / **Charcoal** Direct
Prep time 15 minutes / **Grilling time** 4 to 6 minutes / **Serves** 4

500g fresh tuna
1 small onion
Grated rind of 1 lime
3 tablespoons sweet hot
   pepper (chilli) sauce
Olive oil for brushing
1 small mango, peeled,
   stoned and chopped
1 small bunch of fresh
   coriander, chopped
200ml mayonnaise
4 soft rolls
1 Little Gem lettuce
2 bags root vegetable chips

1. Coarsely break up the tuna, halve the onion and tip into a food processor with the lime rind and sweet hot pepper (chilli) sauce. Blend until smooth.

2. Tip the tuna mixture on to a lightly floured board, and, with lightly floured hands, divide into four portions and shape into patty-shaped rounds. Lightly brush with olive oil and barbecue over Direct High heat for 2 to 3 minutes on each side, turning carefully once.

3. Put the mango in a food processor and blend until smooth. Stir into the mayonnaise with the chopped coriander.

4. Split the rolls in half, arrange the lettuce on the bottom, put a tuna patty on top and serve with root vegetable chips and mango and coriander mayo.

TIP
Try serving these fab tuna patties with – and sometimes without – the roll lid on. It's up to you.

Swashbuckling Swordfish
with Avocado Cream

Gas Direct High heat / **Weber® Q™** Direct High heat / **Charcoal** Direct
Prep time 15 minutes + 15 minutes marinating / **Grilling time** 5 to 7 minutes / **Serves** 2

**2 swordfish steaks,
weighing about 200g
each**
**1 red pepper, seeded and
roughly chopped**
**1 jalapeño pepper, trimmed,
cored, seeded and roughly
chopped**
**3 tablespoons olive oil, plus
extra for brushing**
¹/₂ teaspoon salt

For the avocado cream:
**1 avocado, halved and
stoned**
**3 spring onions, trimmed
and chopped**
**10g fresh coriander,
chopped**
Juice of 1 lime
1 tablespoon olive oil
150ml soured cream

1. Set the swordfish in a large non-metallic dish. Put the red pepper, hot pepper, olive oil and salt in a food processor and blend together, then brush over both sides of the fish. Cover with clingfilm and chill for 15 minutes.

2. Meanwhile, put the avocado, spring onions, coriander and lime juice in a food processor and blend. With the motor still running, trickle in the olive oil and then the soured cream.

3. Remove the swordfish steaks from the marinade (and discard the marinade). Brush the fish with a little oil to prevent sticking, and barbecue over Direct High heat for 5 to 7 minutes, turning once, until cooked through. Serve the swordfish with the avocado cream.

TIP
Tuna or shark steaks can be substituted for the swordfish for a truly tropical feel.

Jamaican Jive Sea Bass
in a Banana Leaf Parcel

Gas Indirect Medium heat / **Weber® Q™** Direct Low heat / **Charcoal** Indirect / **Prep time** 15 minutes + 15 minutes marinating / **Grilling time** 15 to 20 minutes / **Serves** 2

2 sea bass, scaled, gutted and fins trimmed, weighing about 400g each
1 tablespoon Jamaican jerk seasoning
5 tablespoons olive oil
2 large rectanglar-shaped pieces of banana leaf (see Tip below)
Sea salt

For the stuffing:
4 spring onions, trimmed and chopped
2 tomatoes, peeled, seeded and chopped
10cm piece cucumber, cut into strips
Salt and freshly ground black pepper

1. Rinse the prepared sea bass inside and out and pat dry with kitchen paper.

2. Mix together the Jamaican jerk seasoning, salt and olive oil, and rub generously all over the fish.

3. Mix together all the ingredients for the stuffing and use to fill the cavity of the sea bass.

4. Wrap each fish in a single layer of banana leaf and secure with a cocktail stick.

5. Cook over Indirect Medium heat or (or Direct Low for Weber® Q™ gas grills) for 15 to 20 minutes, turning once halfway through. To check the fish is cooked, insert the tip of a knife into the thickest part of the fish, then remove and carefully check to see if the tip of the knife is hot. Serve with boiled green bananas.

TIP
You need a section of banana leaf big enough to wrap each fish. You can find banana leaves, folded into strips, in Chinese and other Asian supermarkets.

Beach-side Peppered Mackerel

Gas Direct Medium heat / **Weber® Q™** Direct Medium heat / **Charcoal** Direct
Prep time 10 minutes + 20 minutes marinating / **Grilling time** 10 to 12 minutes / **Serves** 2

2 whole mackerel, scaled, gutted and fins trimmed, each weighing about 300g
2 tablespoons tropical mixed peppercorns
¹/₄ teaspoon salt
1 large lemon, sliced
Juice of 1 large lemon
2 tablespoons chilli and garlic sauce
Oil for brushing

1. Wash the mackerel inside and out and pat dry with kitchen paper. Set in a large non-metallic dish.

2. Mix together the peppercorns and salt, and sprinkle some in the cavity then over the fish. Fill the cavity with lemon slices. Mix together the lemon juice and the chilli and garlic sauce, and pour over both sides of the fish. Cover with clingfilm and chill for 20 minutes to let the flavours infuse.

3. Brush the peppered mackerel lightly with oil and cook over Direct Medium heat for 10 to 12 minutes or until tender, turning once halfway through cooking.

TIP
In the tropics, peppered pickled mackerel is very popular. Take advantage of the fact that you can get fresh mackerel and make this modern version of the traditional dish.

Sweet & Sour Red Snapper
with Tropical Fruit Salsa

Gas Indirect Medium heat / **Weber® Q™** Direct Low heat / **Charcoal** Indirect
Prep time 15 minutes + 30 minutes marinating / **Grilling time** 15 to 20 minutes / **Serves** 2

**2 red snapper fillets, each
    weighing about 150g**
**Grated rind and juice of
    2 large oranges**
**1 Scotch bonnet pepper,
    trimmed, cored, seeded
    and finely chopped**
1 teaspoon salt
1 teaspoon ground ginger
1 teaspoon tamarind paste

For the tropical fruit salsa:
**2 tomatoes, peeled, seeded
    and chopped**
**2 spring onions, trimmed
    and finely chopped**
**1 green jalapeño pepper,
    trimmed, cored, seeded
    and finely chopped**
**1 teaspoon dark unrefined
    sugar**
**1 small ripe papaya, seeded
    and finely chopped**

1. Rinse the fish inside and out, and pat dry with kitchen paper. Set in a large non-metallic dish.

2. Mix together the orange rind and juice, hot pepper, salt, ginger and tamarind paste, then use to brush liberally inside and out of each fish. Cover with clingfilm and chill for 30 minutes to allow the flavours to infuse.

3. Remove the fish from the marinade (and discard the marinade). Cook over Indirect Medium heat (or Direct Low for Weber® Q™ gas grills) for 15 to 20 minutes, turning once halfway through.

4. Put all the ingredients for the tropical fruit salsa in a bowl and stir together. Serve with the red snapper.

TIP
To check the fish is cooked, insert the tip of a knife into the thickest part of the fish, then remove and carefully check to see if the tip of the knife is hot.

Golden Sunset Sea Bream

Gas Indirect Medium heat / **Weber® Q™** Direct Low heat / **Charcoal** Indirect
Prep time 20 minutes + 15 minutes chilling / **Grilling time** 15 to 20 minutes / **Serves** 2

**2 sea bream, scaled, gutted
and fins trimmed,
weighing about 350g
each**
Juice of 2 limes
**2 teaspoons ground
turmeric**
**1 Scotch bonnet pepper,
trimmed, cored, seeded
and chopped**
4 tablespoons coconut milk
2 tablespoons plain flour
2 tablespoons cornmeal
Olive oil for brushing

1. Rinse the sea bream inside and out, and pat dry with kitchen paper. Set in a large non-metallic dish.

2. Mix the lime juice, turmeric, hot pepper and coconut milk together in a bowl and use to brush liberally inside and out of the fish. Cover with clingfilm and chill for 15 minutes to allow the flavours to infuse.

3. Mix together the plain flour and cornmeal in a shallow dish and roll the fish in this mix. Dab or drizzle with a little olive oil on both sides and cook over Indirect Medium heat (or Direct Low for Weber® Q™ gas grills) for 15 to 20 minutes, turning once halfway through.

Bacardi Fiesta

2 parts light Barcadi rum
**1 part freshly squeezed
lemon or lime juice**
1 part grenadine

Shake ingredients thoroughly in a cocktail shaker with cracked ice. Strain into a chilled old-fashioned glass and serve straight up. Decorate with a slice or lemon and a maraschino cherry.

Garlic Buttered Salmon

Gas Direct High heat / **Weber® Q™** Direct High heat / **Charcoal** Direct
Prep time 15 minutes / **Grilling time** 6 to 8 minutes / **Serves** 4

**4 salmon steaks, each
 weighing about 400g**

For the garlic butter:
**1 tablespoon black mustard
 seeds**
**1 tablespoon yellow
 mustard seeds**
**1 tablespoon unrefined
 sugar**
1 teaspoon all spice
**½ teaspoon dried hot
 pepper [chilli] flakes**
150g butter
3 fat garlic cloves
**4 tablespoons freshly
 chopped coriander**
3 spring onions, chopped
**Salt and freshly ground
 black pepper**

1. Arrange the salmon steaks on a board.

2. To make the garlic butter, grind the black and yellow mustard seeds, sugar, all spice and hot pepper flakes in a pestle and mortar. Add this to a blender with the rest of the butter ingredients and blend together.

3. Melt half the garlic butter and brush liberally over both sides of the fish (discard any leftover melted butter as it has touched raw fish).

4. Cook over Direct High heat for 6 to 8 minutes, turning once halfway through cooking.

5. Put the salmon steaks on a plate, dollop with the remaining garlic butter and serve with a little salad and a portion of brown rice.

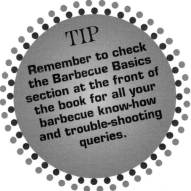

TIP
Remember to check the Barbecue Basics section at the front of the book for all your barbecue know-how and trouble-shooting queries.

CHAPTER THREE

Paradise Poultry

Finger-lickin' West Indian Turkey
with Aubergine Dip

Gas Direct Medium heat / **Weber® Q™** Direct Low heat / **Charcoal** Direct
Prep time 15 minutes + 30 minutes marinating / **Grilling time** 30 minutes / **Serves** 4

500g skinless turkey breast steaks, cut into 2.5cm cubes
1 tablespoon spicy West Indian curry paste
250ml coconut milk
3 tablespoons tomato ketchup
4 spring onions, trimmed and finely chopped
Oil for brushing
Salt and freshly ground black pepper

For the aubergine dip:
2 aubergines
3 garlic cloves
1 green jalapeño pepper, trimmed, cored, halved and seeded
3 tablespoons olive oil
Juice of 2 limes

1. To make the aubergine dip: cut the aubergines in half and season liberally with salt. Put the garlic, chilli and oil in a small food processor and blend briefly, then brush liberally over the aubergines. Cook over Direct Medium heat for 15 minutes, turning once, or until the aubergines are tender. Scoop out the flesh and blend in a food processor with the lime juice. Season to taste with salt and pepper.

2. Tip the turkey cubes into a medium-sized dish. Put the curry paste, coconut milk, ketchup and chopped spring onions in a bowl and stir together, then pour over the turkey cubes and mix well. Cover with clingfilm and chill for 30 minutes to allow the flavours to develop.

3. Thread the turkey cubes on to four metal skewers (and discard any leftover marinade). Brush the turkey with oil and barbecue the skewers over Direct Medium heat (or Direct Low on Weber® Q™ gas grills) for 8 to 12 minutes, or until the turkey is cooked through, turning once halfway through cooking. Serve with the aubergine dip and freshly cooked white rice.

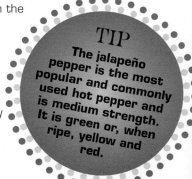

TIP
The jalapeño pepper is the most popular and commonly used hot pepper and is medium strength. It is green or, when ripe, yellow and red.

Jamaican Jerk Chicken
with Red Rice

Gas Direct High heat / **Weber® Q™** Direct High heat / **Charcoal** Direct
Prep time 20 minutes + 25 minutes marinating / **Grilling time** 6 to 8 minutes / **Serves** 4

4 skinless boneless chicken breasts, cut into 2.5cm cubes
180ml jar mild Jamaican jerk marinade
Oil for brushing

For the red rice:
250g red rice
2 tablespoons chopped fresh coriander
Salt and freshly ground black pepper

1. Soak eight wooden skewers in cold water for 30 minutes. Remove them from the water and pat dry before using.

2. Tip the chicken cubes into a shallow dish, pour over the jerk marinade, mix well, cover with clingfilm and chill for 25 minutes.

3. Remove the chicken from the marinade (and discard the marinade). Divide the chicken into eight piles and thread on to the skewers. Brush with oil and barbecue over Direct High heat for 6 to 8 minutes, or until the chicken is cooked through, turning once.

4. Meanwhile, cook the red rice according to the packet instructions, drain, stir in the coriander and season with salt and pepper. Put a portion of rice on each plate and lay two skewers on top.

TIP
Pick up a ready-made jerk marinade – made with spring onions, Scotch bonnet peppers, black pepper, allspice, nutmeg and thyme – in your shop or supermarket.

Spicy Tamarind-glazed Roast Chicken

Gas Indirect Medium heat / **Weber® Q™** Direct Low heat / **Charcoal** Indirect
Prep time 15 minutes / **Grilling time** 1¹/₄ hours to 1¹/₂ hours + resting / **Serves** 4

1.5kg free-range chicken
**2 lemons, halved and cut
    into wedges**
**1 bunch of fresh thyme,
    tied with string**
**2 tablespoons tamarind
    paste**
2 teaspoons Tabasco sauce
2 tablespoons malt vinegar
**2 tablespoons unrefined
    dark brown sugar**
8 tablespoons hot water
**4 garlic cloves, finely
    chopped**
**Salt and freshly ground
    black pepper**
**Lemon and lime wedges, and
    thyme sprigs, to garnish**

1. Liberally season the cavity and the outside of the chicken with salt and pepper, then fill the cavity with lemon wedges and the bunch of thyme. Tie the chicken securely with string so that it stays a good shape during cooking.

2. Using a sharp knife, make small slits in the skin of the bird. Heat all the remaining ingredients together gently in a small saucepan and brush this glaze over the chicken making sure the glaze goes into the slits to flavour the bird (discard any leftover glaze).

3. Put the chicken on a roasting rack and place on the grill. Barbecue over Indirect Medium heat (or Direct Low heat on Weber® Q™ gas grills) for 1¹/₄ to 1¹/₂ hours, or until the juices run clear.

4. Carefully remove the chicken from the grill, cover with foil and leave to rest for 10 to 15 minutes before serving. Garnish with fresh thyme, and lemon and lime wedges.

TIP
Tamarind paste is available in most Asian supermarkets or speciality food stores.

Smouldering Chicken Legs
with Mooli & Coriander Salad

Gas Indirect Medium heat / **Weber® Q™** Direct Low heat / **Charcoal** Indirect
Prep time 10 minutes + 1 hour marinating / **Grilling time** 30 minutes + resting / **Serves** 4

4 chicken legs
¹/₂ teaspoon hot pepper (chilli) flakes
1 tablespoon dried oregano
1 tablespoon dried thyme
Juice of 1 orange
¹/₄ teaspoon ground cumin
4 tablespoons olive oil

For the mooli & coriander salad:
1 large mooli, peeled and cut into fine matchsticks
Juice of 1 lime
2 tablespoons olive oil
3 tablespoons fresh coriander
Salt and freshly ground black pepper

1. Using a sharp knife, cut off any excess fat from the chicken legs, then make deep slashes in the chicken and arrange in a single layer in a large non-metallic dish. Mix together the remaining ingredients and brush over both sides of the chicken legs. Cover and chill for 1 hour.

2. Remove the chicken legs from the marinade (and discard the marinade). Barbecue over Indirect Medium heat for 15 minutes, then turn and cook for a further 15 minutes, or until the chicken legs are tender and the juices run clear. (If using a Weber® Q™ gas grill cook on Direct Low heat for 15 to 20 minutes, then turn and cook for a further 15 to 20 minutes.)

3. Remove the chicken legs from the grill, cover with foil and leave to rest for 5 minutes before serving.

4. Meanwhile, put all the ingredients for the salad in a bowl and stir together. Season to taste with salt and pepper, and serve with the chicken legs.

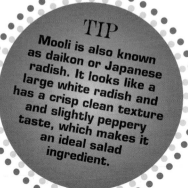

TIP
Mooli is also known as daikon or Japanese radish. It looks like a large white radish and has a crisp clean texture and slightly peppery taste, which makes it an ideal salad ingredient.

Grenadan Spatchcock Baby Chicken
with Five Spice Butter

Gas Indirect Medium heat / **Weber® Q™** Direct Low heat / **Charcoal** Indirect
Prep time 15 minutes / **Grilling time** 30 minutes / **Serves** 2

**2 young chickens or
    poussins, each weighing
    about 450g,
    spatchcocked
100g butter
2 tablespoons five spice
    seasoning
1 teaspoon vanilla extract
1 teaspoon freshly grated
    nutmeg
Salt and freshly ground
    black pepper**

1. Soak four wooden skewers in cold water for about 30 minutes. Remove them from the water and pat dry before using.

2. Using two skewers per baby chicken or poussin, pierce the bird diagonally (in at the wing on one side and out of the leg on the other). Repeat in the opposite direction with another wooden skewer.

3. Melt the butter, five spice seasoning, vanilla extract, nutmeg, and salt and pepper together in a small saucepan and brush on both sides of the baby chickens. (Discard any leftover melted butter.)

4. Barbecue the baby chickens, bone-side down, over Indirect Medium heat (or Direct Low on Weber® Q™ gas grills) for 15 minutes, then turn and cook for a further 15 minutes. Check the juices run clear from the thickest part of the thigh before removing from the grill.

**125ml sparkling apple juice
Ginger ale**

Apple Zinger [non-alcoholic]

Half-fill a highball glass with ice cubes. Pour in the apple juice to ³/₄ fill the glass. Top up with ginger ale. Decorate with a wedge of apple.

Cuban Chicken Thighs
with Sweet Pepper Sauce and Yam Mash

Gas Indirect Medium heat / **Weber® Q™** Direct Low heat / **Charcoal** Indirect
Prep time 25 minutes + 1 hour marinating / **Grilling time** 35 to 40 minutes / **Serves** 4

**8 chicken thighs, weighing
about 200g each**
Oil for brushing

For the sauce:
75ml water
**3 tablespoons unrefined
dark brown sugar**
**2 jalapeño peppers,
trimmed, cored, seeded
and finely chopped**
**1 red pepper, seeded and
finely chopped**
1 large garlic clove, peeled
4 tablespoons lemon juice

For the mash:
**900g yams or sweet
potatoes, peeled and cut
into chunks**
50g butter
**Salt and freshly ground
black pepper**

1. Put the chicken thighs in a large dish. Using a sharp knife, trim off any excess fat and score the skin. Tip all the ingredients for the sauce into a blender and blend until smooth. Pour over the chicken thighs and turn so that they are evenly coated in the sauce. Cover with clingfilm and chill for 1 hour to allow the flavours to develop.

2. Meanwhile, cook the yams or sweet potatoes in a saucepan of boiling water until tender. Drain thoroughly. Mash with butter, season with salt and pepper, and keep warm while you cook the chicken.

3. Remove the chicken from the marinade (and discard the marinade). Brush the chicken with oil and cook, skin-side down, over Indirect Medium heat (or Direct Low on Weber® Q™ gas grills) for 15 minutes. Turn and cook for a further 15 to 20 minutes, or until the chicken is cooked through. Serve with the yam mash and a green salad.

Smothered Chicken Drumsticks
with Rice & Refried Beans

Gas Indirect Medium heat / **Weber® Q™** Direct Low heat / **Charcoal** Indirect
Prep time 15 minutes + 2 hours marinating / **Grilling time** 20 to 30 minutes + resting / **Serves** 4

12 chicken drumsticks
1 onion, finely chopped
3 garlic cloves, finely
chopped
1 teaspoon pepper (chilli)
flakes
1 teaspoon smoked paprika
1 teaspoon dried oregano
4 tablespoons olive oil
Juice 1 lemon
A generous pinch of salt
200g long-grain white rice
seasoned with chopped
herbs and finely chopped
red pepper
2 (215g) cans spicy refried
beans

1. Arrange the chicken drumsticks in a single layer in a large non-metallic dish. Put the onion, garlic, pepper (chilli) flakes, paprika, oregano, olive oil, lemon juice and salt in a food processor and blend, then pour over the chicken pieces. Turn so they are well covered in the marinade, then cover with clingfilm and chill for 2 hours.

2. Remove the chicken drumsticks from the marinade (and discard the marinade). Barbecue the chicken for 20 to 30 minutes over Indirect Medium heat (or Direct Low on Weber® Q™ gas grills) turning once, or until the meat is cooked all the way through. Remove from the grill, cover with foil and leave to rest for 5 minutes.

3. Cook the rice according to the packet instructions, then drain. Heat the refried beans according to the instructions and serve the chicken drumsticks with the rice and beans.

1 part cream sherry
1 part golden rum
1 teaspoon freshly squeezed
lemon or lime juice

Havana Cocktail

Shake the ingredients thoroughly in a cocktail shaker with cracked ice. Strain into a cocktail glass. Decorate with a lemon or lime peel twist.

Caribbean Curried Chicken Breasts
with Turmeric Rice & Spicy Beans

Gas Direct Medium heat / **Weber® Q™** Direct Low heat / **Charcoal** Direct
Prep time 10 minutes + 1 hour marinating / **Grilling time** 10 to 12 minutes / **Serves** 4

- **4 boneless, skinless chicken breasts**
- **3 garlic cloves, crushed**
- **1 Scotch bonnet pepper, trimmed, cored, seeded and chopped**
- **2 tablespoons Caribbean curry powder**
- **1 teaspoon ground cloves**
- **Juice of 2 limes**
- **6 tablespoons light olive oil**
- **200g long-grain white rice**
- **¹⁄₂ teaspoon ground turmeric**
- **1 (420g) can mixed beans in spicy pepper sauce**
- **Chopped fresh coriander, to garnish**

1. Using a sharp knife, make slits in the chicken breasts to allow the flavours to penetrate the meat, and arrange in a single layer in a large non-metallic dish. Put the garlic, hot pepper, curry powder, cloves, lime juice and light olive oil in a blender and blend briefly. Brush this marinade over both sides of the chicken breasts, then cover with clingfilm and chill for 1 hour.

2. Drain the chicken breasts from the marinade (and discard the marinade). Barbecue over Direct Medium heat (or Direct Low on Weber® Q™ gas grills) for 10 to 12 minutes, turning once, or until the breasts are cooked.

3. Cook the rice according to the packet instructions with the turmeric. Heat the spicy beans according to the instructions.

4. Serve the curried chicken breasts, garnished with chopped coriander, with the turmeric rice and spicy beans.

TIP

Caribbean curry powder is a traditional dry-roasted and hand-blended mix of cumin, coriander, fenugreek, black peppercorns, black mustard seed, turmeric and cloves.

Smoked Chilli Duck Breasts
with Mango Salsa

Gas Direct Medium heat / **Weber® Q™** Direct Low heat / **Charcoal** Direct
Prep time 15 minutes + 30 minutes marinating / **Grilling time** 15 minutes + resting / **Serves** 4

4 boneless duck breasts
**2 tablespoons smoked hot
pepper (chilli) jelly**
**1 teaspoon Mauritius
massale spice blend**
A generous pinch of salt
2 tablespoons olive oil

For the mango salsa:
**1 large ripe mango, peeled,
stoned and finely chopped**
**2 spring onions, trimmed
and finely chopped**
**1 red habanero pepper,
trimmed, cored, seeded
and finely chopped**
**5cm piece cucumber, seeded
and finely diced**
**1 tablespoon unrefined light
muscovado sugar**

1. Using a sharp knife, trim the skin off the duck breasts to 3mm and cut off any excess fat that overhangs the edge of the meat. Score the remaining fat into a diamond pattern, cutting right through to the flesh (this helps the excess fat drain away). Arrange in a single layer in a large non-metallic dish.

2. Melt the smoked hot pepper (chilli) jelly, spice blend, salt and olive oil in a small saucepan to make a marinade (be careful; this doesn't take long). Brush the marinade over the duck breasts on both sides so that they are well coated. Cover and chill for 30 minutes.

3. Remove the duck breasts from the marinade (and discard the marinade). Barbecue over Direct Medium heat (or Direct Low on Weber® Q™ gas grills) for 7 to 8 minutes, or until the skin is golden. Turn and cook the breasts for a further 6 to 7 minutes, or until they are just firm to touch (this is medium) or cook for a further 3 to 4 minutes for well done.

4. Put all the ingredients for the mango salsa in a bowl and stir together, then leave to stand while the duck is cooking. Remove the duck from the barbecue, cover with foil and leave to rest for 5 minutes, then serve with the mango salsa.

Rum-soaked Duck Breasts
with Cuban Citrus Sauce

Gas Direct Medium heat / **Weber® Q™** Direct Low heat / **Charcoal** Direct / **Prep time** 15 minutes + 30 minutes marinating / **Grilling time** 10 to 12 minutes + resting / **Serves** 4

8 tablespoons dark rum
1 star anise
1 cinnamon stick, snapped
4 cloves
4 boneless duck breasts

For the cuban citrus sauce:
2 tablespoons olive oil
2 spring onions, trimmed
and finely chopped
2 garlic cloves, finely
chopped
1 teaspoon dried oregano
1 teaspoon ground cumin
100ml orange juice
2 tablespoons fresh
coriander leaves
Salt and freshly ground
black pepper

1. Heat the rum, star anise, cinnamon stick and cloves together in a small saucepan until just boiling, to make a marinade. Leave to cool.

2. Using a sharp knife, trim the skin off the duck breasts to 3mm and cut off any excess fat that over-hangs the edge of the meat. Score the remaining fat into a diamond pattern, cutting right through to the flesh (this helps the excess fat drain away). Arrange in a single layer in a large non-metallic dish, pour over the marinade, cover and chill for 30 minutes.

3. Meanwhile, heat the oil in a frying pan, add the spring onions and garlic, and cook until softened. Add the oregano and dried coriander, and cook for a further 2 to 3 minutes. Add the orange juice, bring to the boil then remove from the heat. Leave to cool. Season with salt and pepper, then stir in the coriander leaves.

4. Remove the duck breasts from the marinade (discard the marinade) and barbecue over Direct Medium heat (or Direct Low on Weber® Q™ gas grills) for 5 to 6 minutes, or until the skin is golden. Turn and cook for a further 5 to 6 minutes, or until they are just firm to touch. Remove the duck from the barbecue, cover with foil and leave to rest for 5 minutes. Serve with the Cuban Citrus sauce.

CHAPTER FOUR

Sizzling
Meats

Creole-crusted Rib-eye Beef

Gas Direct Medium heat / **Weber® Q™** Direct Low heat / **Charcoal** Direct
Prep time 5 minutes + 1 hour marinating / **Grilling time** 30 minutes + resting / **Serves** 4

1.4kg piece rib-eye beef
4 tablespoons hot pepper (chilli) sauce
1 tablespoon ground ginger
1 tablespoon ground cumin
1 tablespoon ground coriander

1. Put the rib-eye beef in a dish. Mix the hot pepper (chilli) sauce, ginger, cumin and coriander together to make a paste, then brush it over the beef. Cover with clingfilm and chill for 1 hour to allow the flavours to infuse.

2. Remove the beef from the marinade (and discard the marinade). Barbecue over Direct Medium heat (or Direct Low on Weber® Q™ gas grills) for 15 minutes, then turn and cook for a further 15 minutes (longer if you like your meat well done). The beef will be rare in the middle and medium on the outside.

3. Remove the beef from the grill, cover with foil and leave to rest for 10 minutes. Serve sliced with fresh crusty bread.

TIP
Leaving meat like this to rest for a few minutes (as long as it is covered and set in a warm place) improves the taste and texture of the meat and makes it easier to carve.

Jerk Beef Burgers

Gas Direct Medium heat / **Weber® Q™** Direct Low heat / **Charcoal** Direct
Prep time 25 minutes + 1 hour chilling / **Grilling time** 10 to 12 minutes / **Serves** 6

1kg lean beef mince
**2 to 3 teaspoons Jamaican
jerk seasoning**
**1 small onion, very finely
chopped**
3 garlic cloves, crushed
6 burger buns
Salt
1 egg
**A few salad leaves and
tomato slices, to serve**

1. Put the minced beef, jerk seasoning, onion, garlic, salt and egg in a large bowl and mix together. Mould by hand into burger shapes, cover with clingfilm and chill for 1 hour to allow the flavours to develop.

2. Using your hands, mould the meat mixture into six burger shapes and barbecue over Direct Medium heat (or Direct Low on Weber® Q™ gas grills) for 10 to 12 minutes, turning once, or until cooked through.

3. Serve in a bun that has been toasted over Direct Medium heat for 1 minute, with a few salad leaves and tomato slices.

Heatwave

5 parts light rum
1 part freshly squeezed lemon juice
1 part raspberry syrup
1 part pineapple syrup

Shake the ingredients thoroughly in a cocktail shaker with cracked ice. Strain into a chilled cocktail glass and serve straight up. Decorate with twists of orange peel and a maraschino cherry.

Beef Salad with a Kick

Gas Direct High heat / **Weber® Q™** Direct Medium heat / **Charcoal** Direct
Prep time 15 minutes / **Grilling time** 4 to 8 minutes / **Serves** 4

4 prime fillet beef steaks, weighing about 200g each
2 tablespoons hot pepper (chilli) oil

For the salad:
2 garlic cloves, crushed
1 red jalapeño pepper, trimmed, cored, seeded and chopped
2 tablespoons soy sauce
2 tablespoons lime juice
2 teaspoons brown sugar
4 handfuls assorted lettuce leaves, washed and drained
Large bunch of fresh coriander, chopped
1 cucumber, peeled, seeded and sliced
Salt

1. Brush the fillet steaks with the hot pepper (chilli) oil and barbecue over Direct High heat (or Direct Medium on Weber® Q™ gas grills) for 2 to 4 minutes on each side, turning once. Remove the steaks from the grill, cover with foil and leave to rest for 5 minutes.

2. Meanwhile, mix together the garlic, hot pepper, soy sauce, lime juice, sugar and salt in a bowl.

3. Arrange the lettuce, coriander and cucumber on four plates. Slice the fillet steaks and add to the salad. Pour over the dressing and serve at once.

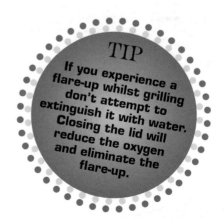

TIP
If you experience a flare-up whilst grilling don't attempt to extinguish it with water. Closing the lid will reduce the oxygen and eliminate the flare-up.

Calypso Beef & Papaya Kebabs

Gas Direct High heat / **Weber® Q™** Direct Medium heat / **Charcoal** Direct
Prep time 10 minutes **Grilling time** 5 to 8 minutes / **Serves** 5

750g sirloin steak, trimmed and cubed
1 tablespoon Gujarati masala
1 papaya, halved, seeded and cut into chunks
Olive oil for brushing
Salt and freshly ground black pepper
Lime pickle, to serve

1. Soak four wooden skewers in cold water for 30 minutes. Remove them from the water and pat dry before using.

2. Toss the cubes of beef in the Gujarati masala in a shallow dish. Thread the beef on to the skewers alternating with the papaya.

3. Brush with olive oil, season with salt and pepper and cook over Direct High heat (or Direct Medium on Weber® Q™ gas grills) for 5 to 8 minutes, turning once. Serve with a dollop of lime pickle.

TIP
To make your own Gujarati masala blend together ajowan seeds, black peppercorns, black cardamom, cloves, cinnamon, coriander seeds, cumin seeds, fennel and sesame seeds and crushed red chillies.

Party-time Hot Pork Ribs

Gas Indirect Medium heat / **Weber® Q™** Direct Low heat / **Charcoal** Indirect
Prep time 5 minutes + 1 hour marinating / **Grilling time** 20 minutes + resting / **Serves** 2

750g pork ribs
2 tablespoons hot pepper (chilli) oil
2 tablespoons dark brown unrefined sugar
Juice of 1 orange

1. Put the pork ribs in a large non-metallic dish. Mix together the hot pepper (chilli) oil, sugar and orange juice and pour over the ribs. Carefully turn the ribs so that they are well coated, then cover and chill for about 1 hour to allow the flavours to infuse.

2. Remove the ribs from the marinade (and discard the marinade). Barbecue over Indirect Medium heat (or Direct Low on Weber® Q™ gas grills) for 20 minutes, turning after 10 minutes, or until cooked all the way through. Cover the ribs with foil and leave to rest in a warm place for 5 to 10 minutes before serving.

Buena Vista

1 part white rum
1 part blue curaçao
1 part sugar syrup
1 part freshly squeezed lime juice

Shake all the ingredients vigorously in a cocktail shaker with cracked ice. Strain into a highball glass. Decorate with a wedge of lemon.

Passion Fruit Soaked Lamb Shanks
with Sweet Potato Mash

Gas Indirect Medium heat / **Weber® Q™** Direct Low heat / **Charcoal** Indirect
Prep time 5 minutes / **Grilling time** 1 hour + resting / **Serves** 4

4 lamb shanks, weighing about 450g each
8 passion fruit, halved and flesh scooped out
3 tablespoons dried wild thyme
Oil for brushing

1. Put the lamb shanks in a dish. Mix together the passion fruit and thyme, and rub liberally all over the lamb.

2. Brush the lamb with oil and barbecue over Indirect Medium heat (Direct Low on Weber® Q™ gas grills) for 1 hour, turning every 10 to 15 minutes. Remove the meat from the barbecue, cover with foil and leave to rest for 10 minutes.

3. Serve with Yam Mash (see page 67) and okra.

Skinny Dipper

2 parts gin
1 part grenadine
1 egg white
1 to 2 teaspoons freshly squeezed lime juice

Shake ingredients in a cocktail shaker with cracked ice. Strain into a chilled cocktail glass and serve straight up with a twist of lime rind.

Butterflied Lamb
with Dark Rum Marinade

Gas Direct Medium heat / **Weber® Q™** Direct Low heat / **Charcoal** Direct
Prep time 10 minutes + 1¹/₂ hours marinating / **Grilling time** 30 to 40 minutes / **Serves** 4

**2kg leg of lamb, butterflied
(see tip below)
150ml dark rum
1 tablespoon freshly grated
nutmeg
1 tablespoon ground
coriander
1 tablespoon ground cumin
Salt and freshly ground
black pepper**

1. Put the lamb in a dish. Mix together the dark rum, nutmeg, ground coriander and ground cumin and rub liberally over the meat. Cover with clingfilm and chill for 1¹/₂ hours, turning occasionally, to allow the flavours to infuse.

2. Remove the meat from the marinade (and discard the marinade) and season with salt and pepper. Barbecue over Direct Medium heat (or Direct Low on Weber® Q™ gas grills) for about 30 to 40 minutes, starting skin-side up, and turning once (longer if you like your meat well done).

TIP
Butterflying – removing the bone and opening out the meat – is a great way of preparing meat for the grill. It means a large cut will cook in a quarter of the time it would take to roast. And it's easier to carve, too!

Allspice Pork Belly

Gas Indirect Medium heat / **Weber® Q™** Direct Low heat / **Charcoal** Indirect
Prep time 5 minutes / **Grilling time** 1 hour + resting / **Serves** 4

1.5kg pork belly
1 tablespoon salt
2 tablespoons ground allspice
4 tablespoons olive oil

1. Score the pork fat in straight lines, following the line of the bone. Rub in the salt and allspice, and brush with the olive oil.

2. Put the meat, skin-side up, on a roasting rack and barbecue over Indirect Medium heat (or Direct Low on Weber® Q™ gas grills) for 1 hour.

3. Remove the meat from the grill, cover and leave to rest for 5 minutes before serving.

2 parts orange juice
2 parts passion fruit juice
¹/₂ part peach schnapps
Champagne or sparkling wine

Passion Fizz

Shake the fruit juices and the peach schnapps vigorously in a cocktail shaker with cracked ice. Strain into a champagne flute and top up with champagne or sparkling wine. Serve straight up with a thin wedge of peach.

Celebration Pork
with Aji Li Mojili Sauce

Gas Direct High + Indirect Medium heat / **Weber® Q™** Direct Medium + Low heat
Charcoal Indirect / **Prep time** 30 minutes + 30 minutes marinating / **Grilling time** 35 to 40 minutes + resting / **Serves** 4

2 **pork tenderloin fillets, weighing about 400g each**
4 **tablespoons fresh pineapple juice**
2 **teaspoons ground ginger**
4 **tablespoons olive oil**
Mixed bean salad and grilled polenta, to serve

For the aji li mojili:
2 **red jalapeño peppers, trimmed, cored, seeded and roughly chopped**
2 **large red peppers, seeded and roughly chopped**
3 **black peppercorns**
3 **garlic cloves**
1 **teaspoon salt**
100ml **fresh lime or lemon juice**
100ml **olive oil**

1. Put all the ingredients for the aji li mojili in a food processor and blend until smooth. Cover with clingfilm and chill until needed.

2. Trim off any excess fat and the silver skins from the pork tenderloins. Make small slashes in the meat. Mix together the pineapple juice and ginger, and pour over the pork. Cover and chill for 30 minutes.

3. Remove the pork from the marinade (and discard the marinade). Brush the pork with olive oil and sear over Direct High heat (or Direct Medium on Weber® Q™ gas grills) for 10 minutes, turning three times. Reduce the heat and cook the pork over Indirect Medium heat for a further 25 to 30 minutes (or for a further 15 to 20 minutes over Direct Low on Weber® Q™ gas grills). Remove the pork from the grill, cover with foil and leave to rest for 5 to 10 minutes. Slice the pork and serve with the aji li mojili, a mixed bean salad and grilled polenta.

Hot Pepper & Garlic Pork Chops

Gas Direct Medium heat / **Weber® Q™** Direct Low heat / **Charcoal** Direct
Prep time 10 minutes, + 1 hour marinating / **Grilling time** 10 minutes + resting / **Serves** 4

3 garlic cloves
1 tablespoon sweet hot pepper (chilli) sauce
1 teaspoon crushed jalapeño pepper
1 teaspoon paprika
1 teaspoon dried oregano leaves
25g fresh parsley
75ml olive oil, plus extra for brushing
4 tablespoons white wine vinegar
4 large pork chops, no thicker than 2.5cm, fat scored at 1cm intervals, each weighing about 350g

1. Put all the ingredients (except the pork) into a blender and blend until smooth.

2. Arrange the pork chops in a single layer in a large non-metallic dish. Pour over the spicy marinade and turn the chops so that they are evenly coated. Cover and chill for 1 hour, turning once.

3. Remove the pork chops from the marinade (and discard the marinade). Brush the chops with oil and barbecue over Direct Medium heat (or Direct Low on Weber® Q™ gas grills) for 10 minutes, turning once halfway through cooking (the exact cooking time depends on how thick your chops are). Remove the pork chops from the grill, cover with foil and leave to rest in a warm place for 5 to 10 minutes. Serve with potato wedges.

TIP
Leaving the pork chops to rest allows the juices to settle and the meat to continue 'cooking' so the internal temperature is perfect when you are ready to eat!

CHAPTER FIVE

Sun-kissed Vegetables

Sweet Potatoes at Sundown
with Sweet Pepper Sauce

Gas Indirect Medium heat / **Weber® Q™** Direct Low heat / **Charcoal** Indirect
Prep time 10 minutes / **Grilling time** 50 to 60 minutes / **Serves** 2

**2 sweet potatoes, total
weight about 500g,
scrubbed**
2 tablespoons olive oil
**280g jar grilled peppers
in oil**
2 garlic cloves, peeled
**1 green jalapeño pepper,
trimmed, cored, halved
and seeded**
**2 tablespoons chopped
fresh coriander**
Salt

1. Brush the sweet potatoes lightly with olive oil, sprinkle with salt and barbecue over Indirect Medium heat (or Direct Low on Weber® Q™ gas grills) for 50 to 60 minutes, or until the sweet potatoes are tender.

2. Drain the grilled peppers, reserving the oil. Tip the peppers into a food processor with the garlic, hot pepper and coriander, and blend to make a paste. Add enough of the reserved grilled pepper oil to make a thick sauce.

3. Split the sweet potatoes, spoon in the sauce and serve at once.

Sea Mist

**3 parts cranberry and
raspberry juice**
3 parts pink grapefruit juice
2 parts vodka
**Slices of lime and lemon
frozen in ice cubes**

Shake the fruit juices and vodka thoroughly in a cocktail shaker with cracked ice. Strain into a highball glass filled with the lemon and lime ice cubes.

Barbecued Tortilla Pick 'Em Ups
with Avocado & Tomato Salad

Gas Direct High heat / **Weber® Q™** Direct Medium / **Charcoal** Direct
Prep time 20 minutes / **Grilling time** 1 minute / **Serves** 4

4 ready-made soft flour tortillas

For the salad:
3 ripe avocados, halved, stoned, peeled and chopped
2 large tomatoes, seeded and chopped
1 serrano pepper, seeded and chopped
1 red onion, chopped
4 tablespoons olive oil
Juice of 2 lemons
4 tablespoons chopped fresh coriander

1. Mix together all the ingredients for the salad and set aside.

2. Cut the tortillas into large triangles and grill over Direct High heat (or Direct Medium on Weber® Q™ gas grills) for 30 seconds on each side. You may find this easier to do in batches.

3. Serve a bowl of the salad with a stack of seared tortilla triangles and let your guests help themselves.

TIP
Serrano peppers are about 5cm long and smooth with a tapered end. They are either red or green with a clean, biting taste. Great for guacamole and salsas!

Stuffed Orange Squash
with Rice & Beans

Gas Indirect Medium heat / **Weber® Q™** Direct Low heat / **Charcoal** Indirect
Prep time 15 minutes / **Grilling time** 40 minutes / **Serves** 4

**4 small round orange
squash, weighing about
400g each**
100g cooked brown rice
**1 (410g) can mixed pulses,
drained and rinsed**
2 tablespoons lime pickle
4 tablespoons coconut milk

1. Remove the tops from the squash and keep the lids. Scoop out the seeds from the centre but keep the flesh intact (if you remove the flesh the squash will collapse on the grill).

2. Put the brown rice, drained pulses and lime pickle in a large bowl. Pour in the coconut milk, mix well and use to fill the squash. Pop the lids back on top.

3. Cook over Indirect Medium heat (or Direct Low for Weber® Q™ gas grills) for 40 minutes, or until tender.

TIP

Do not eat the skin of the squash; and don't worry if it burns a little on the bottom. We're just using the squash as an aromatic – and cute – cooking container!

Castaway Corn with Adobo Butter

Gas Indirect Medium heat / **Weber® Q™** Direct Low heat / **Charcoal** Indirect
Prep time 15 minutes + 30 minutes soaking / **Grilling time** 20 to 30 minutes / **Serves** 4

1 tablespoon ground cumin
A small bunch of fresh
    coriander, leaves chopped
1 tablespoon chopped fresh
    oregano
2 tablespoons chopped
    jalapeño pepper
2 garlic cloves
150g butter
1 tablespoon salt
4 corn on the cobs, with
    husks still attached

1. Put the cumin, coriander, oregano, jalapeño pepper and garlic in a food processor and blend together, then blend in the butter and salt.

2. Soak the corn in plenty of cold water for 30 minutes. Remove the corn and shake to get rid of excess water. Gently peel back the husks without tearing the cob, then remove and discard the silk. Smear the corn with the butter mixture and tie the husks back around the corn. Tie a cotton thread around the top to enclose fully.

3. Arrange the corn on the cooking grate and cook over Indirect Medium heat (or Direct Low on Weber® Q™ gas grills) for 20 to 30 minutes, or until tender, turning once.

Almond Breeze

1 part white rum
Dash of amaretto liqueur or orgeat syrup
¹/₂ part melon liqueur
Tonic water

Shake the rum and liqueurs in a cocktail shaker with cracked ice. Strain into a highball glass, half-filled with crushed ice. Top up with tonic water.

Caribbean Curried Vegetables
with Naan Bread

Gas Direct Medium heat / **Weber® Q™** Direct Low heat / **Charcoal** Direct
Prep time 30 minutes + 1 hour marinating / **Grilling time** 12 to 14 minutes / **Serves** 4

900g prepared mixed vegetables (such as mini-courgettes, halved horizontally; aubergine wedges; red pepper chunks; butternut squash chunks)
Oil for brushing
4 plain naan breads
150ml natural yoghurt

For the curry:
2 teaspoons Caribbean curry powder
3 spring onions, trimmed and finely chopped
4 garlic cloves, finely chopped
8 tablespoons olive oil
1 Scotch bonnet pepper, trimmed, cored, seeded and finely chopped

1. Mix all the ingredients for the curry together in a large bowl. Add the prepared vegetables, toss well and leave to marinate for 1 hour, stirring occasionally.

2. Drain the vegetables (and discard the marinade). Brush the vegetables with oil and carefully arrange them on the grill rack. Cook for 6 to 8 minutes over Direct Medium heat, or until all the vegetable pieces are tender, turning them over once.

3. Remove from the heat, cover with foil and leave to stand while cooking the naan bread on Direct Medium heat (or Direct Low on Weber® Q™ gas grills) for 2 minutes on each side. Serve the vegetable curry with the naan bread and a dollop of natural yoghurt.

TIP
If you want to add a touch of meat to this meal use keema naan breads instead of plain.

Barbecued Plantain Slices
with Mixed Pepper Pickle

Gas Direct High heat / **Weber® Q™** Direct High heat / **Charcoal** Direct
Prep time 30 minutes + several days marinating / **Grilling time** 6 minutes / **Serves** 4

2 plantains, weighing about 250g each
Oil for brushing

For the mixed pepper pickle:
1 aubergine, trimmed and diced
1 large red pepper, seeded and diced
1 large green pepper, seeded and diced
1 large yellow pepper, seeded and diced
1 tablespoon salt
600ml white wine vinegar
2 garlic cloves, crushed
1 Scotch bonnet pepper, trimmed, cored, seeded and chopped
1 cinnamon stick
1 teaspoon bruised coriander seeds

1. To make the pickle, put a layer of vegetables in a large bowl and add a generous sprinkling of salt. Continue layering in this way until all the vegetables and salt for the pickle have been used. Cover with clingfilm and leave to marinate overnight. Next day, rinse the vegetables well and drain thoroughly. Pack in sterilized airtight jars.

2. Put the white wine vinegar, garlic, hot pepper, cinnamon and coriander seeds in a saucepan and bring to the boil. Pour over the mixed pepper mixture in the jars and leave to cool; then cover with airtight lids. Leave for several days to allow the flavours to develop well.

3. Trim both ends of the plantains and remove the skins. Cut into 2.5cm slices on the diagonal, brush with olive oil and cook over Direct High heat for 6 minutes, turning once (the exact cooking time depends on how ripe your plantains are). Serve with the mixed pepper pickle.

Stuffed Aubergines
with Fiery Tomato Sauce

Gas Direct Medium heat / **Weber® Q™** Direct Low heat / **Charcoal** Direct
Prep time 15 minutes / **Grilling time** 15 minutes / **Serves** 4

**2 aubergines, halved
horizontally**
2 tablespoons olive oil
1 onion, finely chopped
2 garlic cloves, crushed
**6 very ripe plum tomatoes,
peeled and roughly
chopped**
**2 teaspoons creole spice
blend**
A little oil for brushing
Salt

1. Scoop out the centre of the aubergines, leaving a rim all the way around so the aubergine does not collapse. Cut a small slice off the bottom so that the aubergine sits flat on the cooking grate.

2. Chop the aubergine flesh and cook in a saucepan with the onion and garlic until softened. Add the plum tomatoes, creole spice blend and salt, and cook until reduced.

3. Brush the aubergine shells with oil, fill with the aubergine mixture, and cook over Direct Medium heat (or Direct Low on Weber® Q™ gas grills) for 12 to 15 minutes, or until the aubergines are tender.

Tropical Lagoon

3 parts clear apple juice
1 part spiced golden rum
¹/₂ part amaretto liqueur
¹/₂ part blue curaçao
**¹/₂ part freshly squeezed
lime juice**

Shake all ingredients thoroughly in a cocktail shaker with cracked ice. Strain into a Boston or highball glass half-filled with ice. Decorate with slices of orange, starfruit, strawberry and a maraschino cherry. Serve with a straw and a parasol.

Chargrilled Tofu with Peanut Sauce

Gas Direct High heat / **Weber® Q™** Direct High heat / **Charcoal** Direct
Prep time 10 minutes, plus 1 hour marinating / **Grilling time** 4 to 6 minutes / **Serves** 4

For the peanut sauce:
2 tablespoons sesame oil
1 small onion, finely chopped
1 mild red pepper, seeded and finely chopped
2 garlic cloves, crushed
2.5cm piece fresh root ginger, peeled and finely chopped
100g salted peanuts
250ml boiling vegetable or chicken stock

For the tofu:
600g firm tofu, drained weight, cut into 1cm slices
1 garlic clove, crushed
1 hot red pepper, seeded and chopped
4 tablespoons hot pepper (chilli) oil
4 tablespoons white wine vinegar
1 small red onion, finely chopped
Chopped fresh coriander, to garnish

1. To make the peanut sauce: heat the sesame oil in a saucepan, add the onion, mild pepper, garlic and ginger, and cook for about 5 minutes, or until softened but not coloured. Add the peanuts, stir gently and heat for about 3 minutes. Add the stock, bring to the boil then simmer for 2 to 3 minutes. Remove from the heat and blend in a food processor or liquidizer until thickened and smooth. Leave to cool.

2. Arrange the tofu slices in a single layer in a large non-metallic dish. Mix together all the other ingredients (except the coriander) and pour over the tofu slices. Cover and chill for 1 hour, turning once.

3. Remove the tofu slices from the marinade (discard the marinade). Barbecue the tofu slices over Direct High heat for 4 to 6 minutes, turning once. Serve at once with the peanut sauce.

TIP

Firm tofu is an excellent protein food suitable for vegetarians and vegans. It absorbs the delicious flavours of spices and herbs during marinating. When grilled, it has a good crisp exterior enclosing the soft centre.

Spicy Sweetcorn Patties

Gas Direct High heat / **Weber® Q™** Direct High heat / **Charcoal** Direct
Prep time 10 minutes / **Grilling time** 2 minutes / **Serves** 4

200g cornmeal
1¹/₂ teaspoons baking
powder
A generous pinch of salt
150ml coconut milk
1 teaspoon Tabasco sauce
1 tablespoon sunflower oil,
plus extra for brushing
2 medium eggs, separated
250g sweetcorn kernels,
thawed if frozen
Plain flour for dusting
Oil for brushing

1. Mix the cornmeal, baking powder and salt together in a large bowl. Add the coconut milk, Tabasco sauce, sunflower oil and egg yolks, and mix well to make a smooth batter.

2. Whisk the egg whites in another bowl until stiff, then fold into the cornmeal mixture together with the sweetcorn kernels. Using floured hands, shape into burger-size fritters. Brush with oil and cook over Direct High heat for 1 minute, then carefully turn and cook for a further 1 minute, or until set. Serve hot.

TIP
You'll find it easier to turn the patties carefully with a long-handled spatula.

CHAPTER SIX

Tropical Treats

Monsoon Mango Wedges
with Coconut Rice Pudding

Gas Direct Medium heat / **Weber® Q™** Direct Medium heat / **Charcoal** Direct
Prep time 10 minutes + 35 minutes to cook the rice / **Grilling time** 3 to 4 minutes / **Serves** 4

250g short-grain white rice
500ml water
1 (400ml) can coconut milk
1 cinnamon stick, broken
2 large firm mangoes
A large pinch of ground allspice
50g butter, melted
Fresh mint sprigs, to decorate

1. Tip the rice into a large saucepan with the water, bring to the boil and simmer for 15 minutes. Add the coconut milk and the broken cinnamon stick, and simmer for a further 15 to 20 minutes, or until the rice is tender and the milk has been absorbed. Remove the cinnamon stick.

2. Peel the mangoes and cut into thick slices around the stone. Season with the allspice and brush with melted butter. Barbecue over Direct Medium heat for 3 to 4 minutes, turning once, to sear the fruit. (The exact cooking time depends on the ripeness and thickness of the mango.)

3. Serve the mango wedges with the coconut rice, decorated with fresh mint.

TIP
This tastes great drizzled with maple syrup.

Five Spice Pineapple
with Lemon Grass Ice Cream

Gas Direct High heat / **Weber® Q™** Direct High heat / **Charcoal** Direct
Prep time 25 minutes + freezing / **Grilling time** 4 minutes / **Serves** 4

For the lemon grass ice cream:
2 tablespoons lemon grass in sunflower oil paste
600ml coconut milk
300ml double cream
6 medium egg yolks
175g unrefined light muscovado sugar

For the pineapple:
8 fresh pineapple rings
100g butter
3 teaspoons five spice seasoning

1. Bring the lemon grass paste and coconut milk to the boil in a small saucepan, stirring continuously. Remove from the heat and leave to cool for 10 minutes to allow the flavours to infuse.

2. Heat the double cream in another saucepan until almost boiling. Whisk the egg yolks and sugar until pale and very thick, then gradually whisk in the hot cream. The mixture should thicken to make a custard. Whisk the coconut milk into the custard mixture and leave to cool. Churn in an ice cream machine. Alternatively, freeze in a freezerproof container until firm and blend in a food processor, then freeze again.

3. Lay the pineapple rings in a non-metallic dish. Heat the butter and five spice in a small saucepan and pour over the pineapple rings, turning once. Barbecue over Direct High heat for 4 minutes, turning once halfway through cooking. Serve with the lemon grass ice cream.

Caramelized Bananas
with Nutmeg & Rum

Gas Direct High heat / **Weber® Q™** Direct High heat / **Charcoal** Direct
Prep time 5 minutes **Grilling time** 8 to 10 minutes / **Serves** 4

**4 large firm bananas, in
their skins
8 teaspoons dark rum
4 teaspoons double cream,
plus extra to serve
¼ teaspoon freshly grated
nutmeg
4 teaspoons unrefined light
muscovado sugar**

1. Cut a thin slice off the bottom of the bananas so that they sit flat on the grill.

2. Make a slit along the top of the banana skins and carefully pour in the rum, cream, nutmeg and sugar.

3. Carefully place the bananas on the cooking grate, slit-side up, and cook over Direct High heat for 8 to 10 minutes, or until the skins are black and softened. Serve the hot bananas with a little extra double cream if wished.

Tijuana Café

**160ml hot black coffee
1 part kahlua or coffee
liqueur
1 teaspoon sugar
3 parts double cream
1 cinnamon stick
Ground cinnamon, to
sprinkle**

Pour the hot coffee into a warm heatproof coffee glass. Stir in the liqueur and sugar then spoon the lightly whipped cream on top so that it floats. Give it a gentle stir with a cinnamon stick and sprinkle with ground cinnamon.

Tipsy Hot Fruit Salad
with Coconut Cream

Gas Direct Medium heat / **Weber® Q™** Direct Medium / **Charcoal** Direct
Prep time 10 minutes / **Grilling time** 10 minutes / **Serves** 4

100g butter
1 teaspoon garam masala
1 tablespoon unrefined soft
light brown sugar
2 bananas, peeled and cut
into chunks
1 papaya, peeled, halved,
seeded and cut into
chunks
1 large mango, peeled,
halved, stoned and cut
into chunks
200g fresh pineapple
chunks
4 tablespoons light rum
300ml whipping cream,
lightly whipped
2 tablespoons desiccated
coconut, toasted (see Tip)

1. Melt the butter, garam masala and sugar in a large aluminium container suitable for use on the barbecue over Direct Medium heat.

2. Add the prepared fruit and rum, toss well in the spiced butter and cook for 10 minutes, stirring and turning once.

3. Divide the hot fruit salad among four dishes and serve with whipped cream sprinkled with toasted desiccated coconut.

TIP

To toast desiccated coconut, put it into a dry saucepan and briefly cook over medium-high heat until golden. Shake the pan frequently so that the coconut colours evenly.

Index

Lucy Knox studied home economics at Surrey University before winning a scholarship to Peter Kump's prestigious cookery school in New York. She is the author of one of the previous books in this series, *Weber's Fun and Easy Grilling* and has worked as a freelance home economist for advertising, books and magazines. In the past she has written regular features for *Best* and the *Express Saturday Magazine*, did a weekly live hour-long cookery programme for BBC Southern Counties radio and has given more than 200 cookery demonstrations at county show throughout Britain. Lucy regularly writes for *Daily Mail Weekend*, the *Sunday Mirror* magazine, *At Home with Lorraine Kelly* and *Now*.